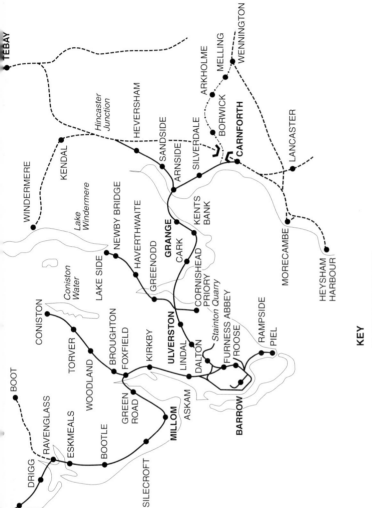

**KEY**

| | | |
|---|---|---|
| ——— | = | FURNESS RAILWAY |
| ⊤⊤⊤⊤ | = | WHITEHAVEN, CLEATOR & EGREMONT RAILWAY |
| ·········· | = | CLEATOR & WORKINGTON JUNCTION RAILWAY |
| ············ | = | FURNESS & MIDLAND JOINT RAILWAY |
| – – – – | = | OTHER RAILWAYS |
| **BOLD TYPE** | = | PRINCIPAL FURNESS RAILWAY STATIONS |

# FURNESS RAILWAY

## A VIEW FROM THE PAST

### HOWARD QUAYLE

Ian Allan PUBLISHING

Dedicated to Tom Clark
'Superintendent of the Line'

First published 2000

ISBN 0 7110 2756 0

© H. I. Quayle 2000

Published by Ian Allan Publishing

an imprint of Ian Allan Publishing Ltd, Terminal House, Shepperton, Surrey TW17 8AS.
Printed by Ian Allan Printing Ltd, Riverdene Business Park, Hersham, Surrey KT12 4RG.

Code: 11/A3

*Front cover:*
The most numerous class of FR locomotives; in the early 1900s, 0-6-0 No 53, built in 1871, heads an up freight along the shores of Morecambe bay, near Grange-over-sands. *From a painting by George Heiron based on a photograph in the Bucknall Collection*

*Back cover, top:*
Furness Abbey station. *RPC*

*Back cover, bottom:*
Furness Railway colour postcards advertising the delights of the lakes. *Furness Railway Trust*

*Endpapers:* A map showing the full extent of the Furness Railway system and its connections in the late 19th century.

*Title page:*
In early LMS days and now sporting a standard smokebox-door number plate, LMS 4-6-4T No 11101 (formerly FR No 116) storms out of Carnforth with a West Cumberland express. Because of their size, these locomotives were nicknamed 'Jumbos'. The tall chimney on the right was on the Carnforth ironworks site. *Kerr Collection, Cumbrian Railways Association*

*This page:*
Behind Class 5MT 4-6-0 No 45294, heading the 09.30 (SO) Barrow–Euston on 18 June 1966, stand Silverdale's Ulverston & Lancaster-designed station buildings. The station was still gas-lit. *B. J. Ashworth*

# Contents

*Below:* Arnside's down side station buildings are of Ulverston & Lancaster design, the wood and brick FR extension in the foreground having been added later. A 1960s view. *Ian Allan Library*

# Foreword

The Furness Railway was always a much more complex undertaking than it appeared at first sight. From its humble origins as a mineral line of only local focus, it grew into a company which controlled not only railways but also mighty industries and docks, and at one point was almost the *de facto* government of the Furness district.

Criticised by some for its parochial outlook and cautious management, the company proved most adept at managing to survive the 'boom and bust' industrial cycles of the mid- to late 19th century, as well as rapidly exploiting the burgeoning tourist industry in the scenic English Lake District. For this latter, it was well placed, with its luxury hotels and its lake steamers, as well as commercially-astute management.

Even after the 1923 Grouping, and Nationalisation in 1948, much of the Furness atmosphere survived, especially in its architecture, and remarkably the main line remains intact today, though the majority of the branches have disappeared and freight traffic — the Furness's original *raison d'être* — is probably at an all-time low.

This book sets out to provide a short history of the company, its locomotives, and the area and industries it served, between its opening in 1846 and absorption into the London, Midland & Scottish Railway (LMS) in 1923. It is not the definitive book on the railway — that has yet to be written — but one which hopefully provides another portrait of a fascinating railway company in one of England's most isolated and beautiful corners.

*Howard Quayle*
Bury St Edmunds, Suffolk
July 2000

*Below:* An FR bridge which never carried a train: although the Bardsea branch, opened in 1883, was intended as the first section of a coastal route to Barrow, rails were never laid on the 7/8 mile of earthworks constructed after the terminus, this double-track-width bridge being the most substantial feature of this long-forgotten section. Pictured on 10 May 2000. *H. I. Quayle*

# 1. Early Years in Furness

The Furness district of Lancashire has long been one of England's most isolated regions, with its hilly terrain compounding traditionally poor communications with the rest of the country. The Lake District mountains to the north prevented the establishment of major trade routes, while Morecambe Bay to the south provided the maritime boundary. Ironically, however, it was the dangerous route across the bay's sands to Hest Bank, near Lancaster, that provided the Furness District with its main link to the rest of England, giving the area its other title: 'Lancashire North of the Sands'.

Probably because of this isolation, the Furness District was not included in any of the earliest railway schemes (between 1825 and 1835). The area was not considered significant economically at the start of the 19th century, iron smelting with charcoal having declined, although there was increasing trade in the export of high-quality haematite iron ore, mined in the Dalton-in-Furness and Lindal areas. Initially exported via the Ulverston Canal (reputedly the 'shortest, widest and deepest canal in England' on its opening in 1796), increasing tonnages were being shipped from the coastal village of Barrow after 1825, when a small jetty was constructed in the Barrow Channel.

With significant tonnages now moving between mines and the Barrow jetty, the mine owners considered the construction of tramways but took this idea no further, and railway activity in the area remained dormant until May 1836 and the promotion of the Maryport & Carlisle Railway. An extension to Lancaster along the Cumberland and Furness coasts, entitled the 'Caledonian, West Cumberland & Furness Railway', was proposed, and in June 1837 the Whitehaven, Workington & Maryport Railway Committee — set up to look into the feasibility of this venture — asked George Stephenson to survey potential routes.

Stephenson acted with a speed that, nearly two centuries later, still looks astonishing. Starting from Lancaster on 1 August, he crossed Morecambe Bay on foot, reaching Ulverston via Humphrey Head.

From here he would have ascended nearly 1,000ft, to the top of Kirkby Moors, descending to cross the Duddon Sands to the hamlet of Millom, before travelling round the base of Black Combe (1,970ft) and up the Cumbrian coast to Whitehaven. Stephenson then moved on to Carlisle, returning south to Lancaster over Shap Fell, and thence to Leicestershire, from where his report was issued on 16 August — just over two weeks after beginning his survey!

The report supported the construction of a piled bank across Morecambe Bay, running from Poulton-le-Sands (later Morecambe) to the vicinity of Bardsea, touching land briefly *en route* at Humphrey Head and Chapel Island. A lengthy tunnel under Lindal Moor would have emerged near Askam, the line then crossing the Duddon Estuary on a further embankment before taking the conventional route, sandwiched between the Lake District mountains and the Irish Sea, north to Whitehaven. Stephenson calculated that nearly 39,000 acres of land would have been reclaimed from the sea as a result.

Alternative plans were also being put forward for a direct Lancaster–Carlisle route, either via Shap Fell or via Kendal and the Kent Valley, although Stephenson's proposals (now known as the 'Grand Caledonian Junction Railway') were increasingly seen as being practical. This seems to have encouraged the Grand Caledonian Junction's supporters to take further Stephenson's broad proposals, and in February 1838 the Provisional Committee of the Caledonian, West Cumberland & Furness Railway appointed the engineer John Hague as the route's official surveyor.

Hague built substantially on Stephenson's original plans, proposing a breathtaking 10-mile 51-chain embankment from Poulton-le-Sands to Goadsbarrow, on the southeast side of the Furness Peninsula, and a further 1-mile 65-chain embankment from Roanhead across the Duddon to Hodbarrow. The line was to be double-tracked, and the scheme was estimated to recover 52,000 acres of land — 33% more than Stephenson's scheme. The cost was a massive £543,000, of

*Left:* A late-19th-century photograph of Piel station, the Roa Island terminus of the service from Barrow. A tank wagon stands on the short siding serving the island's gasworks. The line onto the pier diverged to the left of the picture, about 150yd north of the train shed, to the right of which is the still-extant Roa Island Hotel. *Powell Collection, Cumbrian Railways Association*

which the embankments alone would have amounted to £400,000.

Following a final survey and report by J. M. Rastrick, Hague's scheme was submitted in the 1839 Parliamentary session, together with two other competing schemes to Scotland north of Lancaster — one via Kendal and Haweswater, and the other via the Lune Valley and Tebay (the precursor of the present Shap route). Because of the strategic importance of the Anglo-Scottish corridors to the United Kingdom economy, Parliament ordered the setting up of a Commission to recommend the best route. In May 1840, the Commissioners chose the Shap route, which was not only shorter (68 miles 48 chains between Lancaster and Carlisle, as opposed to 94 miles 45 chains via Hague's coastal route) but also considerably cheaper.

While this decision was probably correct, it denied the 19th century a civil engineering triumph with the magnitude of the 20th century's Channel Tunnel project, and the Furness area an express rail link to the south. Yet Hague's dream was to linger on, in one form or another, for well over a hundred years: a road over a Morecambe Bay barrage was considered in the 1940s, possibly as a postwar development project, while the 1960s saw a proposal to combine a barrage with a wave-power scheme to generate electricity.

While these grandiose schemes were being considered, a much smaller-scale proposal was being drawn up to improve the Furness area's links with the rest of the country, and which, had it gone ahead, would have resulted in the first rails

on the isolated peninsula. In 1835, a steamer service was introduced between Liverpool and the canal pier at Ulverston, which attracted the attention of the Preston & Wyre Railway, the operator of the port of Fleetwood. The P&W, sensing that this market would increase, proposed its own service between the Fylde port and a pier at Rampside, near Piel, from where a branch line would have run to join Stephenson's projected Scottish trunk route in the vicinity of the present settlement of Askam. Nothing came of this 1838 scheme which, had it succeeded, would have pre-dated the first route of the Furness Railway by nearly a decade.

However, this plan came to the attention of London banker John Abel Smith, who, certain that a Furness line would eventually be built, purchased Roa Island in 1840, and proceeded to promote an Act of Parliament to build a deep-water pier on the island and to 'connect Roa Island with the neighbouring island of Great Britain', with a railway laid on a causeway. The Bill became law on 27 June 1843, but no work was to commence for several years, since the jetties in the Barrow Channel (now also used for slate traffic from the Earl of Burlington's slate quarries, as well as for iron ore) were considered to be better sited.

Slowly but surely, pressures were building for some kind of railway in the Furness district, but not along the lines of Stephenson's or Hague's grandiose main-line schemes. As Dr. J. D. Marshall wrote, in *Furness & The Industrial Revolution*, 'The anti-climax was complete. Out of a mountain of imaginative labour emerged a very small mouse.'

# 2. The Furness Railway is Built

The Furness Railway, as originally built, was a short mineral line, linking mines and quarries to local port facilities. Its genesis lay in a survey, commissioned in 1841 by the Duke of Buccleuch and the Earls of Burlington and Lonsdale, from a civil engineer, James Walker, on the shifting courses of the river channels in the Duddon Estuary and in Morecambe Bay, which had a direct impact on property boundaries belonging to these noblemen: Buccleuch owned the Furness ore mines, Burlington the Kirkby slate quarries, and Lonsdale had extensive interests in the Millom area.

To fix the river courses, Walker proposed a series of embankments, some of which could be used for railways. Burlington himself must have already had a railway or tramway in mind when commissioning the report, which speaks of the Dunnerholme (Askam)–Foxfield embankment as being 'suitable for [Burlington's] railway from Kirkby Slate Quarries'. Walker issued his report in August

1842, at the same time that a local surveyor, Job Bintley, was planning the course of a horse-drawn tramway between the Lindal ore-mines and the Barrow jetties.

Although Walker's original plans were not proceeded with, the Duke of Buccleuch and the Earl of Burlington asked Walker and his colleague Alfred Burges to undertake a second survey, on a railway to run between Kirkby-in-Furness (the site of the slate quarries) and Rampside, together with a branch to Barrow and a so-called 'iron-ore railway' linking the Lindal Moor and Stainton mines to a junction at Millwood.

This unambitious and small-scale project had a route mileage of 18 miles 60 chains, and was

*Below:* Kirkby station, some years after the 1904 replacement of the up side buildings, although the platforms remain low-level. The small goods yard (between the goods shed and the station) appears busy. The slate quarries, with their inclines, are on the hills to the right of the up starter. *RPC*

*Left:* The delightfully-rural Furness Abbey station, looking towards the short tunnel. The down loop was used for splitting trains into Ramsden Dock and Barrow portions. The siding on the extreme left, containing two FR ballast-wagons, formerly housed the private saloon of James Ramsden, who lived at nearby Abbots Wood. *RPC*

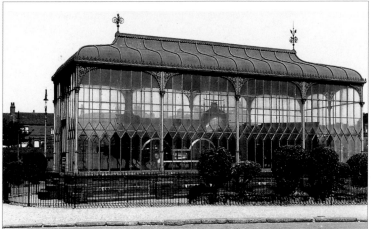

*Below left:* A 1935 view of FR No 3 'Coppernob' in its glass case, adjacent to the Barrow Central approach road. In May 1941, the German bombing raid which wrecked the station also damaged 'Coppernob's' case, after which it was moved to Horwich Works for safe storage. *L&GRP*

*Right:* An 1847 map of Barrow, showing the site of Barrow's original station, which was built close to the site of the FR's later General Offices in St George's Square. Compare this with the map on page 24. *Cumbria Record Office, Barrow*

estimated to cost £100,000. Published in November 1843, the prospectus for the Furness Railway contained few surprises, although the 'iron-ore' railway was replaced by a new line designed to facilitate a further extension to the nearby market town of Ulverston. Despite references in the prospectus to the Furness Railway's becoming 'part of [a] main line of Railway which may…be continued to the North from Fleetwood, by Carlisle and the West Coast of England' (a throwback to Stephenson's and Hague's schemes), the directors were in no doubt that this was primarily a mineral line: 60% of revenue was estimated to come from carrying iron ore, 32% from slate, and only 6% from passenger traffic.

The Furness Railway Bill had a trouble-free passage through Parliament, becoming law on 23 May 1844, with a capital of £75,000 in shares

and £25,000 in debentures. The FR board met for the first time on 17 July, with Benjamin Currey in the chair. Currey was a most influential man, being Clerk of the House of Lords, as well as legal adviser to the Cavendish family, who lived at Holker Hall and who were to play a significant role in later developments.

Construction of the line also seems to have been relatively trouble-free. A contract for construction was signed with W. & J. Tredwell on 12 February 1845, stipulating a single line of rails on a double-track formation. Few physical obstacles were encountered, as, between Roose and Dalton, the line was never more than 100ft above sea level, although a literary problem was encountered in the form of William Wordsworth, whose famous poem beginning 'Well have yon Railway Labourers to THIS ground…' was a protest against the proximity

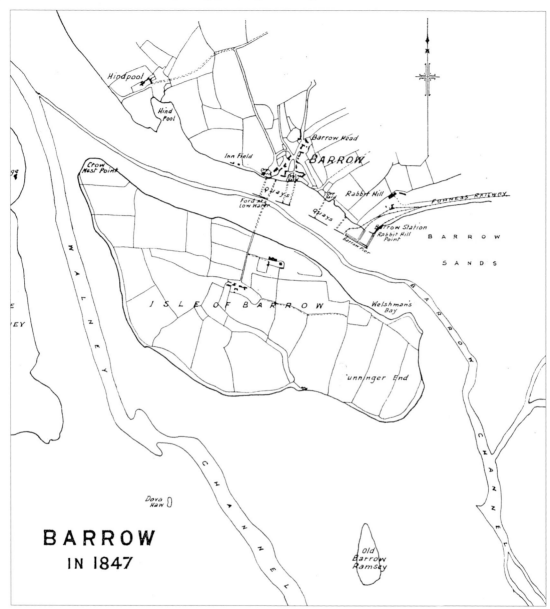

**BARROW**
**IN 1847**

of the new line to the ruins of Furness Abbey. Construction of a short tunnel here may have reduced the poet's wrath!

With construction of the line going well, and with other railways being planned in the vicinity (notably the Whitehaven & Furness Junction), the FR board was already planning modest extensions, to Broughton-in-Furness in the north and to Ulverston in the east. Parliamentary powers were obtained in the

Furness Railway Extension Act of 27 July 1846, although this did not mark the immediate start of an expansionary period for the company; the FR still saw itself as a mineral line. Interestingly, one of the promoters of the bill was John Barraclough Fell of Spark Bridge, who, several years later, patented the Fell system of centre-rail traction, which gave added adhesion on rising gradients and security against derailment on the descent.

At the end of 1845, the FR board ordered the company's first rolling stock — four carriages, 30 side-tipping wagons for iron-ore traffic, 10 slate wagons, and 13 wagons for general use — although the first locomotives, FR Nos 1 and 2, had already been delivered in 1844 for use in the line's construction. These were 0-4-0 bar-framed tender locomotives from the Liverpool firm Bury, Curtis & Kennedy. A further two were ordered in July 1845, being delivered to Barrow by sea in March 1846 and accompanied by 23-year-old James Ramsden, the new Locomotive Superintendent, who later became the FR's General Manager. Nos 3 and 4 on the FR list, these locomotives, with their massive copper-covered fireboxes, survived until 1900 and 1898 respectively, No 3 then being preserved by the Furness itself as the famous 'Coppernob'.

There continues to be some confusion over the precise opening dates for the line, although Marshall quotes contemporary sources in giving 3 June 1846 as the opening of the Barrow–Dalton section for freight and 12 August 1846 for complete opening to all traffic; there is, however, no record of any official opening ceremony. It is not clear whether the FR operated a passenger service from the outset, although, with coaching stock delivered in time for the line's opening, the story that passengers were first carried in a sheep-truck is probably apocryphal!

The most likely main purpose for this stock was to operate services into the Furness hinterland from Piel, connecting with steamers making the crossing from Fleetwood. An agreement between the FR and the previously-mentioned John Abel Smith was drawn up in February 1846, not long after the coaching-stock order was placed, under which Smith would operate the steamers. The FR pushed Smith to complete his causeway between the mainland at Rampside and Roa Island, having undertaken to extend the Piel branch from Concle to Piel Pier on the island. This was completed, and a new Fleetwood–Piel Pier service was set to commence on 24 May 1847.

However, the agreement between the FR and Smith contained nothing about the use of the pier, as a result of which the latter refused to allow passengers to land at this facility, except on terms unacceptable to the FR. It is not certain whether the Piel Pier service actually commenced, as the sailings were transferred to Barrow Pier on 1 June 1847. After much legal action, the FR resumed its boat connections to Piel Pier and the Fleetwood steamer in May 1848, but this episode convinced the FR board to develop its own deep-water berths at Barrow. In any case, the FR had the last laugh, as Piel Pier suffered severe storm damage in December 1852, forcing Smith to sell his property and associated rights to the railway company early in 1853.

# 3. The Railway Expands

Railway Station,

*Above:* Around 1908, the steam railmotor and trailers run into Broughton's passing loop on a Foxfield-bound train. The 1903 waiting room extensions blend harmoniously with the main station building. The almost-empty goods yard, on the right, emphasises the 1 in 49 climb towards Woodland. *RPC*

The early years of the line reflected the conservative and almost insular attitude of the Furness Railway management. All minor extensions in the Dalton iron-ore field required careful financial justification, and passenger traffic was a secondary consideration: in 1848, the directors stated that '…the Mineral and Goods Traffic shall be primarily…provided for, and passenger traffic…only regarded as an auxiliary source of profit…'

Initially there was nothing wrong with this policy. The *Ulverston Advertiser* of 7 February 1850 pointed out that, since the line's opening in 1846, 470,000 tons of mineral traffic had been carried; a staggering achievement, this represented almost 100% of the Furness iron-

ore field's output, although the level of slate traffic from Kirkby was apparently disappointing. The paper also noted that 78,000 passengers were carried in the same period. It was not surprising, therefore, that the first half-year dividend, in February 1847, was 4%, and, even though this was reduced to 2% the following year when a minor depression hit the ore trade, the already-planned extensions went on, the 3-mile 60-chain extension from Kirkby to Broughton-in-Furness opening on 29 February 1848.

1849 saw a resumption of work on the Ulverston extension from Dalton, but of greater significance was the Furness's first link to another railway company, albeit initially in the

## WHITEHAVEN AND FURNESS JUNCTION RAILWAY.

THIS Railway will be OPENED to BOOTLE, for Public Traffic, on MONDAY next, the 1st of July, 1850, on and after which day the Trains will run as follows:—

### DOWN TRAINS.

| STATIONS. | 1 Minrl. & 3d Class. | 2 1st & 2d Class. | 3 1st & 2d Cls. Goods. | 4 1st & 3d Class. | 5 1st & 2d Class. | 1 1st,2d & 3d Class. | 2 1st & 2d Class. | 3 1st & 3d Class. | 1st Class | 2nd Class | 3d Class |
|---|---|---|---|---|---|---|---|---|---|---|---|
| **LEAVE** | | | | | | | | | | | |
| Carlisle | 6 10 | | | 2 30 | | | | | | | |
| Maryport | 7 40 | | | 4 0 | | | | | | | |
| Cockermouth | 7 20 | | | | | | | | | | |
| Workington | 7 56 | | | 4 16 | | | | | | | |
| ARRIVE AT Whitehaven | 8 20 | | | 4 40 | | | | | | | |
| **LEAVE** | A.M. | A.M. | P.M. | P.M. | P.M. | A.M. | P.M. | P.M. | s. d. | s. d. | s. d. |
| Whitehaven | 8 45 | 9 30 | 2 45 | 6 20 | 7 45 | 7 45 | 2 0 | 5 0 | | | |
| St. Bees | 9 5 | 9 43 | 3 4 | 6 36 | 8 0 | 7 59 | 2 15 | 5 14 | 0 8 | 0 6 | 0 4 |
| Nethertown | 9 20 | 9 54 | 3 18 | 6 48 | | 8 9 | 2 25 | 5 24 | 1 6 | 1 2 | 0 7 |
| Braystones | 9 30 | 10 0 | 3 27 | 6 54 | | 8 15 | 2 32 | 5 30 | 1 9 | 1 5 | 0 8½ |
| Sellafield, for Calderbridge | 9 40 | 10 7 | 3 36 | 7 2 | | 8 22 | 2 40 | 5 37 | 2 2 | 1 9 | 0 10½ |
| Seascale, for Gosforth | 9 50 | 10 14 | 3 45 | 7 10 | | 8 29 | | 5 44 | 2 7 | 2 1 | 1 0 |
| Drigg | 10 0 | 10 21 | 3 54 | 7 18 | | 8 36 | | 5 51 | 3 0 | 2 5 | 1 2½ |
| Ravenglass | 10 30 | 10 28 | 4 3 | 7 26 | | 8 43 | | 5 58 | 3 5 | 2 9 | 1 4½ |
| Eskmeals | 10 36 | 10 34 | 4 10 | 7 32 | | 8 48 | | 6 3 | 3 9 | 3 0 | 1 6 |
| ARRIVE AT Bootle | 10 50 | 10 45 | 4 25 | 7 45 | | 9 0 | | 6 15 | 4 5 | 3 6 | 1 9 |
| | P.M. | | | | | | | | | | |
| Broughton (by Coach) | 12 45 | | | | | | | | | | |
| Furness Abbey (by Rail) | 1 35 | | | | | | | | | | |
| Dalton (Ditto) | 1 25 | | | | | | | | | | |
| Ulverston (by Omnibus) | 2 45 | | | | | | | | | | |
| Piel (by Rail) | 1 55 | | | | | | | | | | |
| Fleetwood (by Steamer) | 4 0 | | | | | | | | | | |
| Preston (by Rail) | 6 45 | | | | | | | | | | |
| Manchester (Ditto) | 8 50 | | | | | | | | | | |
| Liverpool (Ditto) | 8 55 | | | | | | | | | | |

*Return Tickets are issued to 1st and 2d Class Passengers at one fare and a half.*

### UP TRAINS.

| STATIONS. | 1 1st,2d & 3d Class. | 2 1st & 2d Cls. Goods. | 3 1st & 2d Class. | 4 Minrl. & 3d Class. | 5 1st & 2d Class. | 1 1st,2d & 3d Class. | 2 1st & 2d Class. | 3 1st,2d & 3d Class. | 1st Class. | 2d Class. | 3d Class. |
|---|---|---|---|---|---|---|---|---|---|---|---|
| **LEAVE** | A.M. | | | | | | | | | | |
| Liverpool | 5 30 | | | | | | | | | | |
| Preston | 7 15 | | | | | | | | | | |
| Fleetwood | 9 0 | | | | | | | | | | |
| Piel | 11 0 | | | | | | | | | | |
| Ulverston | 10 30 | | | | | | | | | | |
| Dalton | 11 20 | | | | | | | | | | |
| Furness Abbey | 11 30 | | | | | | | | | | |
| Arrive at Broughton | 12 15 | | | | | | | | | | |
| Leave Broughton | 2 15 | | | | | | | | | | |
| **LEAVE** | A.M. | A.M. | P.M. | P.M. | | A.M. | P.M. | P.M. | s. d. | s. d. | s. d. |
| Bootle | 7 0 | 11 30 | 4 35 | 4 45 | | 9 15 | | 7 15 | 0 8 | 0 6 | 0 3 |
| Eskmeals | 7 12 | 11 45 | 4 45 | 5 3 | | 9 25 | | 7 25 | 0 11 | 0 9 | 0 4½ |
| Ravenglass | 7 18 | 11 52 | 4 50 | 5 12 | | 9 30 | | 7 30 | 1 4 | 1 1 | 0 6½ |
| Drigg | 7 26 | 12 2 | 4 57 | 5 24 | | 9 37 | | 7 37 | 1 9 | 1 5 | 0 8 |
| Seascale, for Gosforth | 7 34 | 12 11 | 5 4 | 5 36 | | 9 44 | | 7 44 | 1 9 | 1 5 | 0 8½ |
| | | | | | | | P.M. | | | | |
| Sellafield, for Calderbridge | 7 42 | 12 20 | 5 11 | 5 48 | | 9 50 | 4 0 | 7 50 | 2 2 | 1 9 | 0 10½ |
| Braystones | 7 50 | 12 29 | 5 18 | 6 0 | | 9 57 | 4 8 | 7 57 | 2 7 | 2 1 | 1 0½ |
| Nethertown | 7 56 | 12 36 | 5 24 | 6 9 | | 10 4 | 4 15 | | 2 11 | 2 4 | 1 2 |
| | | | | | P.M. | | | | | | |
| St. Bees | 8 20 | 12 50 | 5 35 | 6 26 | 8 15 | 10 15 | 4 25 | 8 15 | 3 7 | 2 10 | 1 5 |
| Arrive at Whitehaven | 8 30 | 1 10 | 5 50 | 6 50 | 8 30 | 10 30 | 4 40 | 8 30 | 4 5 | 3 6 | 1 9 |
| **LEAVE** | A.M. | | P.M. | | | A.M. | | | | | |
| Whitehaven | 9 30 | | 6 20 | | | 6 0 | | | | | |
| Workington | 9 54 | | 6 44 | | | 6 24 | | | | | |
| Maryport | 10 10 | | 7 0 | | | 6 40 | | | | | |
| Arrive at Cockermouth | 10 20 | | 7 20 | | | 8 16 | | | | | |
| Arrive at Carlisle | 11 40 | | 8 35 | | | 8 10 | | | | | |

*Return Tickets are issued to 1st and 2d Class Passengers at one fare and a half.*

Season Tickets are issued to 1st and 2d Class Passengers between St. Bees and Whitehaven, the Terms for which may be known at the St. Bees and Whitehaven Stations.

The following Coaches run in connexion with the Trains, viz.:—From Bootle to Broughton, at 10 45 A.M.; Fares, 4s. 6d. inside; 3s. 3d. outside; returning from Broughton at 2 15 P.M.

Conveyances from Calderbridge will meet No. 2 down, and No. 3 up Trains, on Week Days; and No. 2 down, and No. 3 up Trains, on Sundays, at Sellafield.

Passengers may Book at the Whitehaven and Bootle Stations to Broughton, Furness Abbey, and Ulverston; and at the Steam Packet Office, Ulverston, to Broughton, Bootle, and Whitehaven.

Ravenglass, 27th June, 1850.

BY ORDER.

*Left:* Whitehaven & Furness Junction Railway timetable for July 1850. Note that, by this period, the line had been extended to Bootle (Cumberland). *Cumbria Record Office, Barrow*

*Centre right:* Bootle station in British Rail days, looking north towards Eskmeals. The wooden crossing gates have been replaced by a non-standard design, although the Furness Railway signalbox and the goods shed (on the extreme right) still remain; the latter has been converted into a private house. *Cumbrian Railways Association Collection*

*Bottom right:* The up side at Millom station, probably taken in the mid-1930s. In the early years of the 20th century, the FR added the ornate canopy to the original structure, whose steeply-pitched roof can just be seen beneath the rear supports. *Shillcock Collection, Cumbrian Railways Association*

form of a coach connection. Both the Maryport & Carlisle and the Whitehaven Junction Railway (linking Maryport and Whitehaven) already provided an unbroken rail link between the 'Border City' and the chief port on the Cumberland coast, and in 1844 plans were made to extend south to join the FR. Once again, George Stephenson was involved, persuading the Earl of Lonsdale that he needed a southern rail outlet for his Whitehaven coal mines, to run down the coast to the Millom area, and thence across the Duddon Estuary on an embankment to Dunnerholme (Askam) and a junction with the Furness — Stephenson's 1837 scheme was still refusing to lie down.

Incorporated by two Acts (in July 1845 and August 1846), construction of the Whitehaven & Furness Junction Railway began early in 1847, and by July 1849 had reached Ravenglass, from where a coach connected with the FR's Broughton terminus. However, the Duddon embankment had by now been dropped on cost grounds, and the line continued from the Millom area along the shores of the Duddon, bridging the river near Foxfield, whence it continued to Broughton, the rails of the W&FJ and the FR running side by side for the last mile.

Opened throughout on 1 November 1850, the W&FJ advertised through journeys between Carlisle and Piel Pier (for the South), although passengers had to walk between the Whitehaven termini at Preston Street and Bransty until the 1333yd-long Corkickle tunnel

*Right:* A 1947 view of Ravenglass and its staggered platforms, looking towards Whitehaven. Two FR 'squirrel' seats are visible on the down platform, whose buildings are now a public house, the 'Ratty Arms'. *L&GRP*

made true through-running possible in 1852. At the opening ceremony for the W&FJ, Lord Lonsdale mentioned a possible extension from Broughton to Coniston, for moving copper-ore traffic to the Barrow wharves, but more important was his expressed wish for a line from Ulverston to a junction with the Lancaster & Carlisle Railway, which had been open to passengers since December 1846.

Lonsdale may well have had contact with the L&C board, which, in 1850, indicated its interest in an Ulverston–Lancaster line 'with a

view to bringing iron ore in that direction'. However, the major promoters of a link between Ulverston and the L&C were the Brogden family, who already had ore-mining rights in the Stainton area and who were amongst the earliest shareholders in the FR. The conservative railway company, still attempting to complete the Crooklands-Ulverston link through Lindal tunnel, showed little interest in promoting the line itself, baulking at the prospect of having to construct long viaducts across the treacherous Leven and Kent

*Left:* St Bees station, the main crossing loop on the single-line section between Sellafield and Whitehaven (Mirehouse Junction), showing the attractive red sandstone building on the up side and the Furness waiting shelter on the down. The gable end wall adjacent to the footbridge carries an FR station sign, and this still exists, having been restored in the 1990s.
*Shillcock Collection, Cumbrian Railways Association*

*Below left:* Whitehaven Corkickle station in LMS days, looking towards the southern portal of the 1,333yd-long Whitehaven tunnel. When re-lining of the single-track bore became necessary in 1932, possession was only available for a short period each night, and the task was not completed until 1958! Note the three-armed down outer home signal for Whitehaven Bransty, just to the left of the portal. *Pattinson Collection, Cumbrian Railways Association*

*Above right:* The FR signalbox at St Bees, seen here in March 1969, controls the adjacent level crossing, as well as the passing loop, and, with its tapered base, is almost identical to the box at Park South. *S. C. Dent*

*Right:* An FR survivor: at the north end of the 1,333yd-long Whitehaven tunnel, beneath the canopies of Bransty station, stands the Whitehaven Corkickle up fixed distant, photographed in 1936.
*Ian Allan Library*

estuaries, but the Brogden faction and its supporters pushed on, the Ulverston & Lancaster Railway Bill becoming law on 24 July 1851.

Trouble lay ahead for both undertakings. On the FR, the first contractor for the Ulverston extension went into liquidation, while the second proved little better, being accused of shoddy workmanship. Local landowners were holding out for high prices, whilst new port construction in Barrow was diluting labour supplies. As a result, the Ulverston extension was still a mile short of its destination in 1853, with the first mineral traffic not running into the market town until April 1854. The official opening took place on 7 June the same year, although the imposing high-level terminus (which still survives today, after many years as a goods depot) was not completed until the

year-end. The construction of the Ulverston extension had been an engineering feat, with its tunnel (at 250ft, the highest point on the Furness main line), its sinuous curves and its 1 in 76 gradients, but these features were themselves to pose operating problems in the coming years.

Engineering difficulties were also being encountered on the Ulverston & Lancaster, notably in the construction of the Leven and Kent viaducts. The initial engineers were replaced by James Brunlees, whose expertise in constructing railway embankments on the River Foyle, near Londonderry, made him an ideal choice. These technical difficulties, which centred on the method of pile-driving, were compounded by financial problems, which drove the Brogdens to seek support from the FR board early in 1856. Initially lukewarm, the

*Left:* Ulverston station in August 1965. Now-preserved Class 2MT 2-6-0 No 46441 is about to leave for Lakeside, having run round its train from Morecambe. A corner of the original Furness terminal can be seen in the top right, together with the steps which led down to the low-level Ulverston & Lancaster platforms. *W. H. Foster*

*Below left:* The Kent viaduct on 10 April 1950, with Class 4MT 2-6-4T No 42429 heading the 14.05 Carnforth–Barrow. The main span over the river channel can be clearly seen beneath the second and third vehicles. *W. S. Garth*

*Bottom right:* Cark in Cartmel station in FR days, with Ulverston & Lancaster buildings on the down side and Furness buildings on the up. Note the Furness-design 'squirrel-end' seat on the right, and the advertisement for 'K Boots' (the forerunner of K Shoes) on the left. *Kerr Collection, Cumbrian Railways Association*

directors had a total change of mind later in the year, when proposals were announced to build a trans-Pennine route — the South Durham & Lancashire Union Railway — with the aim of linking 'the coal and ironstone on the East with the ports and manufactures of the West'. Seeing for the first time that their line could be a major link in a coast-to-coast freight-orientated rail system, the FR directors advanced £50,000 for the completion of the U&L on 11 December 1856.

Thereafter, completion of the Ulverston to Carnforth link was relatively rapid, the wooden viaducts over the Leven and Kent estuaries being completed on 14 June and 24 July 1857

respectively. By this time, most of the remainder of the route, including the picturesque sea-wall section on the western side of the Kent, had already been completed, and the Ulverston & Lancaster was opened to passengers on 26 August 1857, freight traffic having commenced a few days earlier. The company's independence was short-lived, however, the FR absorbing the Ulverston company in 1862, together with the Ulverston Canal, whose already-declining traffic was now killed off by the new line.

The opening of the U&L brought significant advantages to Lancashire North of the Sands.

*Above:* With Grange's down starter in the right background, No 9, one of Pettigrew's 0-6-0s, runs along the sea wall towards Kents Bank. This may be an empty stock working, as the locomotive — not normally a passenger type — is displaying a pick-up goods headcode. *L&GRP*

*Below:* Carnforth in LNWR days: the Furness platform is on the left, with the London–Glasgow platforms on the right. The overall roof was demolished in the late 1930s when a second Furness line platform was constructed. *L&GRP*

*Right:* Park South signalbox, at the northern end of the Barrow avoiding line, is one of a handful built by the Furness in the 1880s, the tapering base and steep roof being its most distinguishing features. In this 1960s view, grimy Class 9F 2-10-0 No 92051 approaches Thwaite Flat crossing and is about to take the Barrow avoiding line to Dalton Junction with an up freight from West Cumberland.
*Ward Collection,*
*Cumbrian Railways Association*

*Below right:* In September 1954, Fowler Class 4MT 2-6-4T No 42364 stands at Foxfield with a Barrow–Millom local. Only down side passengers had the benefit of an overall roof, but the island platform was provided with covered waiting accommodation. The small goods shed abuts the adjoining trainshed.
*Ian Allan Library*

A link to the national rail network at Carnforth provided speedier access to the rest of the country, even though the line was more circuitous than Stephenson's grand proposals, and replaced the dangerous route across the sands. Excursions began almost immediately, and were well patronised: on 24 May 1858, a Whitehaven–Lancaster excursion carried 1,400 passengers. In anticipation of the opening of the trans-Pennine route from County Durham, with its plentiful supplies of coke, three blast furnaces were erected in Barrow in 1859, and by the time the South Durham route was opened to its junction with the Lancaster & Carlisle (now leased to the London & North Western Railway) in July 1861, three more had been constructed. There was now a continuous line of rails round the Furness and Cumberland coasts, but schedules were not helped by the reversals needed at Furness Abbey and at Broughton. As a result, two short sections of line were built, the east-to-north Millwood Curve (now part of the Barrow avoiding line) bypassing Furness Abbey and the south-to-west Foxfield Curve eliminating the Broughton reversal.

The greater part of the Furness Railway network was now complete; the next decade was to see the start of some important strategic alliances.

# 4. Prosperity and Alliances

The success of the Furness Railway in the 1860s was based upon the local availability of high-grade haematite iron ore, limestone and Henry Bessemer's discovery of the semi-steel process. Local speculator H. W. Schneider had discovered a massive haematite seam at Park, which by 1856 was producing 120,000 tons per annum, while plentiful limestone deposits existed in the Stainton district southeast of Dalton.

The Furness Railway, whose directors were closely associated with both the local ore mines and the iron foundries, benefited enormously from this industrial expansion: in 1863, the company carried 600,000 tons of haematite and 250,000 tons of coal and pig-iron over its 59 route-miles, and had become massively profitable, its dividend rising from 7.5% in 1860 to 9.5% in 1866. Its nearest rival among the so-called 'Bessemer' lines — small Cumbrian systems with mainly haematite iron-ore traffic — was the Whitehaven, Cleator & Egremont company, which paid out a massive 13.5% in 1863, but had dropped back to 9% by 1866. Net receipts, too, increased out of all proportion to the district's iron-ore output, rising from £40,000 in 1860 (when the mines produced

521,000 tons) to £199,000 ten years later (when ore output had only increased to 872,000 tons). This reflected the fact that the Furness had metamorphosed from being a local ore transporter, into a link to the national network, despatching haematite to Yorkshire and the Midlands, and bringing in coal and coke for use in the furnaces.

As many of the FR shareholders, such as the Duke of Buccleuch and the Earl of Burlington, also had controlling interests in the related local enterprises such as the vast Park ore mine, capital was readily available for other economic development in the Furness district. The FR board, therefore, now drew up a clear long-term strategy, centred on Barrow and on its sea frontage, which was already in the FR's property portfolio.

The hamlet of Barrow, with its population in 1841 of 250, had become a large village of 3,135 inhabitants by 1861, rising to nearly 20,000 by 1871. By dint of careful planning, the FR strategy was to create a new port complex, rivalling Liverpool to the south, around which new industries would be created to complement the existing foundries: raw and semi-finished materials would arrive over

*Left:* The abandoned Carnforth Station Junction signalbox, with the Furness & Midland Joint bay in the background, at the time of the 1930s rebuilding. The alcove above the windows on the gable end contains the Cavendish coat of arms. *L&GRP*

Furness metals, with finished goods being despatched by sea, or alternatively these moves would be reversed. James Ramsden — by now the FR's General Manager — planned this complex around the 'new' town of Barrow, which (according to S. Pollard and J. D. Marshall) was to be 'an industrial colony…[with] wide streets [and] a civic and market centre'.

It was also Ramsden who initiated discussions with the Midland Railway about possible joint use of the planned Barrow docks. The expansionary Midland had already reached Poulton-le-Sands (Morecambe) via the 'Little' North Western railway from Skipton, but had found the tide-dependent Poulton Harbour of limited use for its Irish and Isle of Man steamer services. The prospect of deep-water facilities at Barrow appealed to the Midland directors, some of whom visited the FR offices in September 1862 to discuss a new 10-mile link between Wennington and Carnforth, which would allow the transfer of the Midland's Irish traffic to Barrow. As a result, two schemes — the Furness & Midland Railway Bill and the Barrow Harbour Bill — were submitted to Parliament in March 1863, becoming law on 22 June the same year.

However, construction of the F&M line was part of a hidden agenda for the Midland — direct main-line access to Scotland — and it seems that there were three attempts to pursue this aim. Firstly, the opening of a branch, in 1861, between the Lancaster & Carlisle (now on a 900-year lease to the London & North Western Railway) to an end-on junction with the Midland at Ingleton appeared to provide the desired facility, but the poor quality of connections provided by the Euston company made this arrangement unworkable. Secondly (although this would have provided a very circuitous route) the MR tried unsuccessfully, in 1864/5, to negotiate a joint lease of the L&C with the LNWR, but once again the latter held the upper hand.

The third option was the F&M. Although, by the time that the Wennington link was under construction, the Midland was actively surveying the famous Settle to Carlisle route, this was clearly an expensive alternative, and the MR must have hoped that a unified Cumberland coastal line, combined with a resurrected Duddon crossing and a planned Solway viaduct, would be the key to an independent Scottish trunk line.

At this stage came a series of developments which once again illustrated the parochialism of the Furness board. Perhaps with one eye on the Midland's perceived plan, the Whitehaven & Furness Junction proposed a new Duddon crossing, from Hodbarrow to Dunnerholme (Askam), with a Bill deposited in September 1864. There is some evidence that the Whitehaven company hoped that the Furness would combine this shortened crossing with a new trunk line from Barrow to Ulverston,

*Right:* Askam station in 1910, with a down passenger train just leaving. The scene here is little changed today, although the goods shed has now been demolished. At the north end of the up platform was a short spur, used by the banking locomotive to provide assistance up to Lindal Summit. *RPC*

*Below:* Furness Railway signalling: Millom's down home, with its repeater arm and, lower down, shunt signal. The lattice girder post, with its distinctive finial, is typical of the first generation of FR signals. The top arm displays the typical early-FR filigree-type decoration between the spectacles, while the lower represents a later, simpler FR pattern. Winched lamps appear to have been replaced by fixed ones, two ladders having been attached to the post.
*Shillcock Collection, Cumbrian Railways Association*

running along the Morecambe Bay coast, and thus eliminating the steep gradients over the backbone of the Furness Peninsula, but the FR board refused to discuss this. As a result, in October 1864, the W&FJ proposed a direct line from Dunnerholme to Lindal, through a 2-mile 20-chain tunnel, bypassing Barrow and its new port completely. The 1837 Stephenson scheme was still refusing to lie down.

Alarmed at these developments, the FR now proposed its own Duddon crossing, a much longer route from Hodbarrow to Roanhead, whence a short line, passing just south of the Park mine, would have connected with the existing route. When, in March 1865, Parliament found in favour of the W&FJ proposals, the Furness was placed on the defensive, and responded by purchasing the W&FJ in June of the same year.

Now came the FR's fatal mistake. Possibly because of arguments over price, it refused the Whitehaven Junction Railway's offer to sell, failing to see the wider consequences of not acquiring this critical link in the coastal chain. The LNWR pounced immediately, buying the WJ which it reached over the metals of the Cockermouth, Keswick & Penrith and Cockermouth & Workington railways. Having tracked with some concern the Midland's covert plans for the Scottish route, the LNWR (to quote the words of a local historian) now

*Left:* The FR lattice post later gave way to a square wooden design, similar to that used on the LNWR. This example, with its later design of signal arm, was photographed on the southern approaches to Barrow Iron & Steel Works at Hindpool. Some survivors of this type were still in use in the early 1970s, controlling connections into the Vickers shipbuilding and engineering complex on Barrow Island.
*Shillcock Collection, Cumbrian Railways Association*

'had the Furness in the nut-crackers', as it controlled the FR's northerly and southerly outlets. Although the FR gained its access to the Midland network when the Furness & Midland line opened on 6 June 1867, and although the steamer services were transferred, the Furness had been trumped: no great 'Scotch expresses' would traverse the Furness Peninsula, and the FR still had a Parliamentary obligation to construct the Duddon viaduct.

On the positive side, the commodious new docks at Barrow were formally opened on 19 September 1867 by Prime Minister W. E. Gladstone, who remarked during his speech: 'Some day, Barrow will become a Liverpool'. To James Ramsden, now Barrow's Mayor as well as the FR's Managing Director, these words must have represented the high-point of his great career — words which, sadly, were later never to be realised. Nonetheless, with its external ambitions thwarted, it was Barrow docks which provided the Furness with much of its commercial focus in the latter decades of the 19th century.

With the railway company's finances in good shape, and its cash reserves increasing, the FR board decided to push ahead with the Duddon viaduct, in the hope of carrying a significant proportion of the Hodbarrow mines' haematite output, which had now reached 140,000 tons a year. Work recommenced in 1867, and sections of ironwork for the bridge were cast, but capital expenditure, particularly for renewals and track doubling, was becoming excessive, and this, together with the realisation that the system would now never become part of a trunk line, persuaded the FR to apply for a

Duddon Viaduct Abandonment Bill in May 1869. This was granted by Parliament only on condition that the Askam–Millom fare be based on the distance across the estuary — three miles — and not on the more circuitous 6½-mile route via Foxfield. This curious fare structure remained in place for many years. Even today, a short length of approach embankment on the Duddon foreshore near Askam survives — one tiny section of what could have been a Stephenson masterpiece.

By 1870, the Furness Railway system was substantially complete, apart from minor extensions such as the completion of the Barrow line (opened from Barrow's Strand station to Ormsgill in 1873) and the Arnside–Hincaster connection, which was seen by the Durham industrialists as a useful short-cut to the Barrow furnaces, and by the LNWR as a useful link from the north into Furness territory. The Furness itself displayed little enthusiasm until the Euston company exerted the pressure, and work on the 5-mile 26-chain link began in July 1874. Completion in June 1876 provided the Furness with running powers to Kendal.

Ramsden's grand plan for the FR was working as the 1860s came to an end. A minnow in terms of route mileage — 109 miles 28 chains — was generating traffic receipts of £478,000 and profits of £230,000 in 1870. As forecast, the railway was carrying ore to the local ironworks and taking away the finished products, as well as servicing the growing number of new industries being established on railway-owned land in Barrow. It looked as though there was to be no holding back the success of the Furness Railway.

# 5. Good Times and Bad Times

*Left:* The General Offices of the Furness Railway, adjacent to St George's Square in Barrow, shortly before demolition in 1978. The buildings were in continuous railway use from 1855 until the merger of British Rail's Barrow and Preston divisions in 1966. The central clock tower was originally topped by an Italianate belfry, while the carved lintel on the window above the archway *(left)* commemorates final completion of the building in 1864. *Headech Collection, Cumbrian Railways Association*

*Left:* An 1873 map of Barrow Docks, showing the FR's station on the Strand, with its adjacent carriage shed. Note the expansion of the rail network onto the adjacent Barrow Island.
*Cumbria Record Office, Barrow*

BARROW DOCKS
IN 1873

*Right:* One of 30 three-plank wagons built around 1880, No 4057 was photographed in 1930 still bearing its Furness Railway initials. *L&GRP*

*Below right:* Barrow Central station with its magnificent overall roof, taken not long after the 1902 preservation of FR No 3 'Coppernob' in its glass case on the left. An unidentified FR locomotive can just be seen on the reversible Platform 1. *LPC*

At the start of this period, in the words of Pollard and Marshall, in their paper *The Furness Railway and the Growth of Barrow*, 'the Furness Railway Company had ceased to be a transport organisation pure and simple. It was the *de facto* government of Barrow…'. Ramsden's plan was bearing more fruit, in the joint venture between the railway company and the local ironworks, Schneider & Hannay, resulting in the creation of Britain's biggest steel company, the Barrow Haematite Steel Co, which, by 1872, was capitalised at more than £1,000,000 and paying dividends of 30%.

Convinced that it could build on the joint ventures concept, and urged on by the mini-boom of the early 1870s, the FR further refined its strategic plan, which had a number of strands, the main ones being:

• additional investment by the railway company in existing local industry;
• development of Barrow-based shipping companies;
• additional docks, together with increased warehousing;
• introduction of a shipbuilding industry.

As usual, the Furness began to implement its plans with vigour, with Ramsden, the Duke of

Devonshire and other railway and steelworks directors selecting a site, in February 1870, on Barrow Island for the shipyard, to be known as the Barrow Shipbuilding Co. Ramsden and Devonshire also set up the Eastern Steamship Co, to operate a service between Barrow and India, and supported the formation of the Barrow Ocean Steamship Co, to operate sailings to Canada. Following the opening of the Devonshire Dock in 1867, a second — the Buccleuch Dock — was opened in 1873; these facilities allowed increased exports from the expanding steelworks, as well as grain imports to the newly-opened Steam Corn Mill and timber imports to the new merchants on Barrow Island.

Vigour itself, however, was not enough. The isolated nature of the Furness Peninsula was always a negative factor in attracting and retaining new industry, and the start of the Great Depression in 1874 was to hit the area very severely. The shipbuilding company narrowly avoided liquidation, and was only rescued by more capital investment by the Duke of Devonshire. The port of Barrow — by now one of the largest in the UK — saw further expansion, in the form of the new Ramsden dock, yet handled only half the tonnage of the much smaller Grimsby.

*Above:* Immaculate FR 4-4-0 No 36 stands beneath the trusses of Barrow Central's overall roof. To the right of the station official, in his pillbox hat, the shape of Barrow carriage sheds is just visible. The train is possibly a Millom–Carnforth local. *Kerr Collection, Cumbrian Railways Association*

*Below:* Map of lines (open/closed/projected) in the Barrow area.

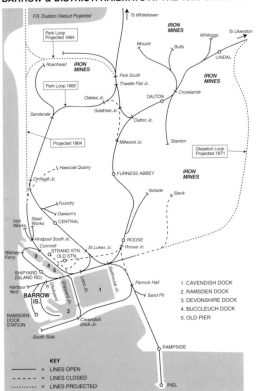

**BARROW & DISTRICT: RAILWAYS AT THE 1923 GROUPING**

The railway company itself, however, when divorced from the activities of its joint-venture partners, fared rather better, and continued to improve its network. The main addition was the construction of the Barrow Loop, from Salthouse Junction, near Roose, to Ormsgill Junction, where the earlier freight lines serving the docks and other heavy industries trailed in from the left. The FR's tendency to over-commit to new capital projects meant that the new line, started in 1871, was not completed until June 1882, when the commodious new Barrow Central station, with its glazed overall roof, replaced the Strand station opened only 20 years previously. This greatly eased access to Barrow from the north, one result being the demotion of what was now the Barrow avoiding line (from Park South Junction to Dalton Junction) to virtually freight-only status.

An indication that further large-scale capital investment in new FR lines could not be justified came with two other proposals from this period. A plan for a new direct line between Lindal and Barrow docks — the so-called Gleaston Loop — was eventually downgraded to a single-track freight branch to Stank iron-ore mines (although traffic levels of 35–40 freights a day between Lindal and

Barrow were causing main-line congestion), while the resurrected plan for a more-easily-graded main line along the shores of Morecambe Bay came to no more than a short branch from Plumpton Junction to Conishead Priory, opened in June 1883; however, earth- and bridge-works, continuing for a short distance beyond the priory towards Bardsea, were constructed, and still exist today.

In the north of the FR's territory, some tidying-up of the Cumbrian rail network took place in 1879, with the joint acquisition of the Whitehaven, Cleator & Egremont Railway by the Furness and the LNWR, the FR handling all traffic apart from specified freight services. By this time, however, the directors of the railway company, whose fortunes had tumbled dramatically through their joint-venture losses, had already made one attempt to sell the company to the Midland or the LNWR, in 1875, but neither was interested, and a further attempt at a sale, in 1882, was equally unsuccessful.

After 1881, two negative factors combined to depress further opportunities for FR expansion: the effects of the nationwide depression on Barrow's industries and docks, and the gradual exhaustion of the local iron-ore reserves. Ample proof of the first is provided by looking at the accounts of Barrow docks, where the value of exports fell from £1.5 million in 1882 to £609,000 five years later; evaluated imports fell from £636,000 to £389,000 in the same period. Yet Ramsden and the FR board continued to invest in new facilities, both for the railway and the docks. In June 1881, Ramsden Dock station was opened for the Isle of Man steamers, with the Belfast boats transferring four months later. This meant closure of the direct route from Roose and the abandonment of Piel Pier station, so bitterly fought over only three decades previously. With this closure, a small piece of the Furness Railway passed into oblivion.

Time was now running out for the first generation of Furness industrialists — Schneider, Devonshire, Ramsden and their associates. To quote from Marshall, 'these men…[now] had grounds for knowing that their efforts to put Barrow at the centre of a web of world trade had met with…failure'. Little by little, the FR's industrial interests were abandoned, the corn mill being sold in 1881 and

*Above:* A view from the never-commissioned bridge near Bardsea, looking back towards Conishead Priory station, hidden behind the trees left of centre. It is clear that the formation was intended for double track, although the Conishead Priory branch remained single. Pictured on 10 May 2000. *H. I. Quayle*

the financially-disastrous shipyard being rescued as the Naval Construction & Armaments Co in 1888, before finally being sold to Vickers, Sons & Maxim nine years later. After control of the Haematite Steel Co had passed to investors outside the Furness area, the interests of the FR were finally centred on railway and closely-related activities.

The Duke of Devonshire died in 1891, and Sir James Ramsden, having been forced to retire as the FR's Managing Director in 1892, passed away in October 1896. His final failure was the Midland Railway's decision, in 1893, to withdraw its Belfast and Manx steamer services

*Left:* The Whitehaven, Cleator & Egremont's main junction station at Moor Row, looking east in early BR days. The signalbox, of LNWR design, was tall enough to provide a good view of the Egremont line as it curved in sharply from the south.
*Headech Collection, Cumbrian Railways Association*

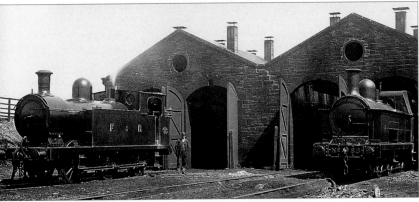

*Below left:* The sandstone-built four-road engine shed at Moor Row, around 1920. On the left is one of Pettigrew's capable 0-6-0Ts, No 57 (renumbered from 21 in 1918), while on the right is 0-6-0T No 83, built in 1863 and showing the tapered modified cabsides fitted unofficially at Moor Row.
*LPC / Bucknall Collection*

*Below left:* Moor Row engine shed in March 1950. On the left stands ex-LMS Class 2P 4-4-0 No 406 (by now officially BR No 40406), while in the centre stands ex-LMS Class 3F 0-6-0T No 47390. An unidentified '3F' 0-6-0 stands on the right. *Ian Allan Library*

*Bottom left:* Although closed to regular passenger traffic, apart from workmen's services to Sellafield, Moor Row station sees activity on 3 September 1953, as Class 4F 0-6-0 No 44461 awaits departure for Sellafield and connection with a Morecambe excursion. The seven-coach rake is ex-North Staffordshire Railway stock.
*W. A. Camwell*

*Right:* Egremont's compact station, looking south and pictured after the passenger closure date of 7 January 1935. Workmen's services continued to operate between Whitehaven, Moor Row and Sellafield until September 1965, and the main buildings (here with a canopy) were still in existence in 1980, when freight traffic from the nearby iron-ore mines was finally withdrawn. *Headech Collection, Cumbrian Railways Association*

*Right:* One of six composite third/first class coaches built in 1882, FR No 57 was photographed in 1908. *L&GRP*

*Below:* Furness Railway map of Barrow Docks and rail connections, as in 1895. *Cumbria Record Office, Barrow*

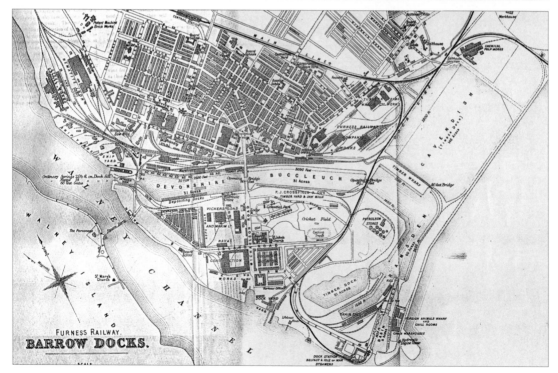

FURNESS RAILWAY.
**BARROW DOCKS.**

## FURNESS RAILWAY.
## List of Signal Boxes, and Hours of Duty.

| Distance to Signal Box in Advance. | Method of Working. | Switch. | SIGNAL BOX. | Week Days From | To | Sundays From | To | REMARKS. |
|---|---|---|---|---|---|---|---|---|
| M.C. | | | **MAIN LINE.** | | | | | |
| 0.25 | Block | | Carnforth St'n. Jn. | Always | | | | Closed after return of Mail Engine on Sundays until 5-0 p.m. |
| 2.78 | " | | F. & M. Jn. | Always | | | | |
| 2.47 | " | | Silverdale | 4 30 | 11 0 | Closed | | |
| 1.59 | " | | Arnside | 4 30 | 10 15 | Closed | | |
| 1.28 | " | | Meathop {Summer/Winter} | 9 0 / Closed | 7 0 | Closed | | |
| 1.67 | " | | Grange | 4 20 | 11 15 | Closed | | |
| 2.30 | " | | Kents Bank {Summer/Winter} | 8 15 / 8 30 | 6 45 / 6 0 | Closed | | |
| 2.2 | " | | Cark | 4 45 | 10 30 | Closed | | |
| 1.51 | " | | Ravensbarrow {Summer/Winter} | 9 0 / 8 45 | 7 0 / 6 30 | Closed | | |
| 0.37 | " | | Leven Junction | — | — | — | | Opened as required. |
| 1.44 | " | | **Plumpton Junction** | 4 20 | 11 30 | 4 10 a.m. | 9 0 p.m. | |
| 0.23 | " | | Ulverston East | 4 45 | *9 30 | 1-0 to 3-0 p.m. Summer. | | *11 45 p.m. on Fris. & Sats. |
| 1.57 | " | | " West | 4 45 | *11 0 | 4 45 p.m. / †5 45 p.m. (†8-30 p.m. Summer.) | | *11 45 p.m. on Fris. & Sats. |
| 0.56 | " | | Lindal East | 4 40 | *11 0 | Closed | | * Or until last Goods Train. |
| 0.34 | " | | " West | 5 0 | 10 30 | Closed | | |
| 1.7 | " | | " Station | 9 30 | 11 0 a.m. | Closed | | |
| 0.19 | " | | Crooklands | 8 15 | 5 45 | Closed | | |
| 0.56 | " | | Dalton Station | 4 30 | 12 5 mid. | 4-30 a.m. to 9-0 p.m. | | |
| 0.74 | " | | " Junction | 5 0 | 10 45 | Closed | | |
| 1.60 | " | | Furness Abbey | 5 0 | 9 45 | Closed | | |
| 0.47 | " | | Roose {Summer/Winter} | 8 45 / 9 0 / 1 0 | *6 45 / 11 0 a.m. / 2 30 p.m. | Closed | | *9-30 p.m. on Saturdays. |
| 0.27 | " | | Salthouse Junction | 4 30 | 12 0 mid. | *12 15 p.m. | 12 45 p.m. | *Summer |
| 0.68 | " | | St. Luke's Junction | 4 15 | *12 5 mid. | 4 45 a.m. | †9 10 p.m. | *12-25 mid. Sats. †10-30 p.m., Summer. |
| 0.12 | " | | Central South {Summer/Winter} | 5 0 / 5 0 | *11 0 / †10 0 | 1-30 p.m. | 9-30 p.m. Summer. | *12-15 a.m. on Thurs. & Sats. †11-0 p.m. on Sats. |
| 1.1 | " | | Central North | 4 15 | *12 5 mid. | 5 0 a.m. | †9 30 p.m. | *12-20 mid. Sats. †10-30 p.m., Summer. |

It is necessary for Boxes shown in heavy type to be open for all Trains, Ordinary or Special.

| Distance to Signal Box in Advance. | Method of Working. | Switch. | SIGNAL BOX. | Week Days From | To | Sundays From | To | REMARKS. |
|---|---|---|---|---|---|---|---|---|
| | | | **MAIN LINE**—Continued. | | | | | |
| 1.10 | " | | Ormsgill Junction | 8 15 a.m. | *5 25 p.m. | Closed | | * 4 0 p.m. Sats. |
| 1.41 | " | | Sandscale | — | — | — | — | Opened as required. |
| 0.39 | " | | Park South | 4 40 | Last booked train. | *Closed | | *Gates worked by Gateman on Sundays. |
| 0.59 | " | | " North | 6 0 | 9 30 | Closed | | |
| 0.59 | " | | Askam Iron Works | 12 15 p.m. | 1 30 | Closed | | |
| 3.16 | " | | **Askam Station** | 4 20 a.m. | *10 30 | 5 0 a.m. | †7 35 p.m. | *12 15 mid. Sats. †9 0 p.m. Summer |
| 2.20 | " | | Kirkby {Summer/Winter} | *10 0 / *10 0 | 7 30 / 4 0 | Closed | | *7 0 a.m. Thurs. |
| 1.74 | " | | **Foxfield** | 4 30 | *10 50 | 5 15 a.m. | †7 35 p.m. | *12 5 mid. Sats. †8 40 p.m. Summer. |
| 2.43 | " | | Green Road {11 45 / †8 30} | *5 45 / 9 30 a.m. | Closed | | | *6 30 p.m. in Summer. †Thursdays only. |
| 3.6 | " | | Millom | 4 40 | *10 0 | Closed | | *12 mid. Sats. |
| 5.24 | " | | Silecroft | 8 45 | 6 55 | Closed | | |
| 2.5 | " | | Bootle | 5 0 | 9 45 | 5 30 a.m. / 5 0 p.m. | 10 40 a.m. / 8 20 p.m. | |
| 0.73 | " | | Monkmoors | 7 0 | 11 30 a.m. | Closed | | Opened at other times as required. |
| 1.37 | " | | Eskmeals | Closed | | Closed | | |
| 2.5 | " | | Ravenglass | 7 55 | 6 0 p.m. | Closed | | |
| 1.76 | " | | Drigg | 8 35 | 6 45 | Closed | | |
| 2.3 | " | | Seascale {Summer/Winter} | 7 45 / *2 0 | 6 0 / 3 30 | Closed | | *Also 8 15 to 9 40 a.m. on Thurs. |
| 3.40 | Tablet | | **Sellafield** | 5 30 | 9 35 | 5 30 a.m. / 5 30 p.m. | 10 50 a.m. / 8 35 p.m. | |
| 2.64 | " | | Nethertown | 6 0 | 10 0 | 6 0 a.m. / 5 30 p.m. | 11 0 a.m. / 8 40 p.m. | |
| 3 20 | " | | **St. Bees** | 6 0 | 10 5 | 6 0 a.m. / 5 30 p.m. | 11 5 a.m. / 8 45 p.m. | |
| 0.25 | Block | | Corkickle / **Mirehouse Jun.** | 5 0 | 10 5 | 6 30 a.m. / 5 15 p.m. | 11 10 a.m. / 8 45 p.m. | |
| 0.76 | Tablet | | **Preston St. Jun.** | 5 0 | 10 45 | 6 30 a.m. / 5 15 p.m. | 11 45 a.m. / 9 15 p.m. | |
| — | " | | Whitehaven **Bransty No. 1** | 5 0 | 10 45 | 6 30 a.m. / 5 0 p.m. | 11 30 a.m. / 9 30 p.m. | |

It is necessary for Boxes shown in heavy type to be open for all Trains, Ordinary or Special.

from the relatively new Ramsden Dock, although delays in completing the commodious Heysham Harbour delayed the transfer until September 1904. Thereafter a residual steamer service from Ramsden Dock lingered on until the outbreak of war in 1914. Dividends were also suffering, falling from 7.25% in 1882 to a paltry 1.5% in 1892.

Despite the deaths of Devonshire and Ramsden, control of the FR was to remain within 'the family'. Devonshire's son, the Marquess of Hartington, had already succeeded his father as Chairman in 1887, and Ramsden's own son, who had joined the company in 1881, also assumed a managerial role. It was to be this new generation who would appoint the man destined radically to change the Furness Railway over the following two decades.

*Above:* From one of the later FR Rules & Regulations Books: the opening hours of FR signalboxes. Note that, with the exception of Carnforth F&M and Station Junctions, no FR box was continuously open. *Cumbria Record Office, Barrow*

# 6. The Aslett Era

Alfred Aslett, who was appointed as the Furness Railway's Company Secretary in August 1895 and promoted to General Manager in 1897, is perhaps the best-known figure associated with the line.

His background, as Company Secretary and General Manager of the Cambrian Railways, was well suited to reviving the FR's fortunes. With a railway system whose competitor controlled both northern and southern outlets, where passenger facilities had become run down, and whose freight traffic was in decline,

*Right:* Furness Railway colour postcard advertising the Lake District with a view of Lake Windermere c1905. *Furness Railway Trust*

*Below:* The steam yacht *Gondola* was launched in October 1859, for service on Coniston Water. Described by *The Illustrated London News* as 'the most elegant little steam vessel yet designed', *Gondola* was in regular service until September 1939. Having sunk in 1962, she was later raised and fully restored, re-entering service in June 1980. *Bucknall Collection / Ian Allan Library*

Aslett had to change completely the FR's strategy. Aided by the growth of annual family holidays among the general population, he vigorously promoted tourism in the Lake District and the Furness area. The timing was perfect; to quote Marshall, 'No longer were the Lakeland dales a preserve of the

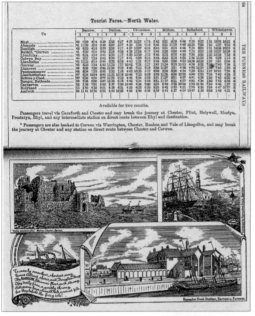

leisured…sections of society; ever wider sections of the British public were beginning to find the value of walking shoes…and climbing tackle…'.

Although the Furness already had extensive experience of operating steamers (the *Lady of the Lake* had been operating on Lake Windermere as early as 1845, and the now-famous *Gondola* on Coniston Water since 1860), and therefore could be considered to be a tourism pioneer, having published 128-page holiday guides since 1886, it was Aslett who made tourism the FR's main priority. The trips and holidays on offer were many and varied, but were centred around no fewer than 20 combined road and rail (and, in some cases, sea) tours: for example, the tourist could cross from Fleetwood to Barrow by fast paddle-steamer, take the train to Lake Side, then appreciate the magnificent scenery from the deck of a Windermere steamer; from Ambleside, a horse-drawn coach would take the visitor to Coniston, via Skelwith Bridge, and from Coniston, a direct train to Barrow made the connection into the Fleetwood steamer. The cost of this trip was 7/6 (37½p)!

For longer breaks, Aslett promoted golfing and angling holidays, combined with stays in Furness-area hotels such as Conishead Priory and Furness Abbey, the latter belonging to the

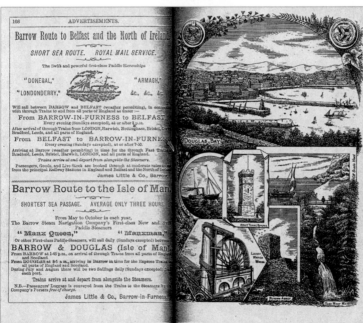

*Above left & left:* For several years, from 1886 onwards, the FR published a 128-page booklet entitled *The Furness Railway's Tourist & Excursion Season.* These two reproductions show the quality of the mono engravings with which the book was illustrated — Ramsden Dock station, Douglas Bay and Piel Castle can be seen — as well as the usual information on train fares and steamer sailings.
*Cumbria Record Office, Barrow*

FR, where 'the roof of the entrance hall is a reproduction of that at Bury St Edmunds Abbey, and the frieze of the coffee shop is copied from the frieze work at St Alban's Abbey'; no expense was spared in making this one of the country's finest provincial hotels. Publicity also became important, with many free pamphlets distributed, together with a large number of attractive postcards showing watercolours of Lakeland scenes; today these have become much sought-after collectors' items. The FR publicity machine was also instrumental in developing some of the smaller seaside villages into railway-served resorts. Chief among these was Grange-over-Sands, beautifully sited between Cartmel Fell and the shores of Morecambe Bay, where the railway tracked the coast in a fashion similar to the Great Western Railway at Dawlish, and which was now marketed as the 'Torquay of the North'. Arnside, too, benefited from its position on the Kent Estuary. Perhaps the only failure

*Below:* FR 0-6-0 No 16 drifts through Furness Abbey station on a down express goods in the early 1900s. The 36-bedroom Furness Abbey Hotel is on the left, while the tall signalbox is just visible above the train's second vehicle. *Ian Allan Library*

*Below:* Publicity material for the FR's celebrated 'Twenty Tours', as published in April 1902. The most expensive — No 15, at 12/- — was an exceptionally long itinerary, and usually meant an overnight stay in Keswick or Penrith.
*Cumbria Record Office, Barrow*

## FURNESS RAILWAY.

### TWENTY COACH AND STEAM YACHT TOURS

. . THROUGH THE . .

### English Lake=Land

#### Daily during June, July, August and September.

No. 1.—**Outer Circular Tour,** embracing Windermere Lake, Furness Abbey, and Coniston. Fare from 8/3.

No. 2.—**Inner Circular Tour,** embracing Furness Abbey, Coniston Lake (Gondola), and Crake Valley. Fare from 3/3.

No. 3.—**Grange and Windermere Circular Tour,** embracing Grange, Arnside, Kendal, and Windermere Lake. Fare from 2/9.

No. 4.—**Middle Circular Tour,** embracing Windermere Lake, the Crake Valley, and Coniston Lake. Fare from 4/9.

No. 5.—**Red Bank and Skelwith Force Tour,** via Ambleside and Skelwith Force, returning via Rydal Water. Fare from 2/9.

No. 6.—**Thirlmere, Grasmere, and Windermere Tour,** via Ambleside, Clappersgate, and Red Bank, and round Thirlmere Lake. Fare from 5/-.

No. 7.—**The Four Lakes Circular Tour,** viz., Coniston, Grasmere, Rydal, and Windermere. Fare from 5/9.

No. 8.—**Coniston to Coniston Tour,** via Red Bank, Grasmere, and Ambleside, returning by Coach to Coniston. Fare from 4/6.

No. 9.—**Tarn Hows Tour,** via Ambleside and Coniston, returning by Tilberthwaite and Elterwater. Fare from 4/6.

No. 10.—**Round the Langdales and Dungeon Ghyll Tour,** via Ambleside, Colwith Force, Grasmere, and Rydal. Fare from 5/-.

No. 11.—**Ullswater Tour,** via Ambleside, Kirkstone Pass, and Brothers Water, returning via the Vale of Troutbeck and Lowwood. Fare from 5/6.

No. 12.—**Derwentwater (Keswick) Tour,** via Ambleside, Grasmere, and Thirlmere. Fare from 6/-.

No. 13.—**The Five Lakes Circular Tour,** viz., Windermere, Rydal, Grasmere, Thirlmere, and Derwentwater. Fare from 11/6.

No. 14.—**Wastwater Tour,** via Seascale and Gosforth. Fare from 4/6.

No. 15.—**The Six Lakes Circular Tour,** viz., Windermere, Rydal, Grasmere, Thirlmere, Derwentwater, and Ullswater. Fare from 12/-.

No. 16.—**The Duddon Valley Tour,** via Broughton-in-Furness, Ulpha, and Seathwaite. Fare from 3/9.

No. 17.—**The Round of Coniston Lake,** new Tour. Fare from 3/10.

No. 18.—**Ennerdale Lake and Calder Abbey Tour,** via Seascale, Gosforth, and Cold Fell. Fare from 4/6.

No. 19.—**Across the Ferry Tour,** via Lake Side, Eathwaite Water, Hawkshead, and Storr's Hall. Fare from 3/6.

No. 20.—**Cartmel Priory and Newby Bridge Tour,** via Windermere (Lake Side), Backbarrow Falls, Holker Park, and Grange. Fare from 3/-.

For further particulars see "**Tours through Lakeland.**" Pamphlets to be had gratis at all Furness Railway Stations; of Mr. F. J. Ramsden, Superintendent of the Line, Barrow-in-Furness; at Messrs. Thos. Cook & Sons' and H. Gaze & Sons' offices; and the Polytechnic Institute, Regent Street W.; or Messrs. W. H. Smith & Son's principal Bookstalls, price 4d.

The **New Palette Album,** illustrating above Tours, in colours, can be obtained at the principal Railway Bookstalls, price 6d.

**Barrow with Fleetwood for Blackpool,** per Paddle Steamer "**Lady Evelyn.**"—During the Summer Months the Furness Railway Company's new Paddle Steamer, "Lady Evelyn," will sail daily between Barrow and Fleetwood for Blackpool. For further particulars as to Sailings and Fares, etc., see announcements. Luncheons, Teas, and Refreshments provided on board.

Barrow-in-Furness,
*April,* 1902.

ALFRED ASLETT,
Secretary and General Manager.

127

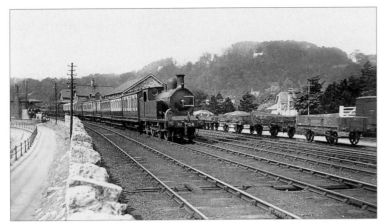

*Left:* FR 0-6-2T No 104 leaves Grange with a 10-vehicle up train; the first six coaches are Furness stock. The date is probably c1910.
*L&GRP / Bucknall Collection*

*Centre left:* In the early years of the 20th century, No89 FR 0-6-0 heads a Millom–Carnforth relief working out of Grange. Note the prominent headboard.
*L&GRP / Bucknall Collection*

*Below:* Seascale, looking south in LMS days, in 1936. To the right-of-centre background, the FR signalbox can just be made out, while to the left a line of coaches stands in front of the large goods shed. The yard here was lower than the main line, and housed camping-coaches until at least 1970. *RPC*

*Right:* At the isolated Braystones station, on the single-line section between Sellafield and Whitehaven (Corkickle), the Furness line runs almost at sea level before ascending, through the cliffs in the distance, to the next station, at Nethertown. In this 1930s photograph, the Stationmaster stands in front of the single platform. The up and down home signals, on an FR lattice post, were operated from a ground frame.
*Pattinson Collection, Cumbrian Railways Association*

*Right:* Dating from around 1894/5, FR Brake Third No 13 — one of six built — was photographed in 1908. *L&GRP*

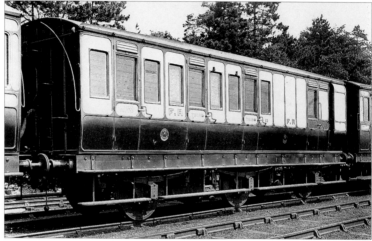

was at Seascale, on the Irish Sea coast, which never expanded as much as the Furness would have wished, perhaps because of its more exposed situation.

With FR policy focusing on passenger traffic, passenger numbers grew by more than 100% during the 18 years after Aslett's appointment. In 1910, the system carried more than 3 million passengers, many of whom had been attracted by Aslett's policy of cheap day tickets at the single fare for the return journey. This marketing strategy, introduced as an experiment in the summer of 1896, was extended to all services, on an 'all-year-round' basis, in January 1898. There was, however, a price to pay for this new and increasing traffic. With many of its capital assets (with perhaps the exception of its stations) having been neglected in the previous two decades, new

investment was needed, and William F. Pettigrew, appointed as Locomotive, Carriage & Wagon Superintendent in 1896, was charged with designing new locomotives and more modern passenger rolling stock. The latter was electrically lit — the first so equipped in northern England — and replaced Midland Railway rolling stock on the Leeds/Bradford services which still worked to Barrow over the F&M line. Most of these services continued to divide at Furness Abbey station into portions for Ramsden Dock (for the Belfast boats) and Barrow Central, until this practice ceased in 1904, when Heysham Harbour opened, with Barrow's consequent loss of the majority of the Irish traffic.

Apart from tourism, there were several other developments on the FR during this period. The short section of the original Kirkby–Piel

Pier line between Goldmire and Millwood Junctions, little used since the opening of the Barrow Loop in 1882, was finally closed in 1898. Millwood Junction signalbox survived long after closure of the line, since the railway author O. S. Nock, who moved to Barrow in 1916, recalls it as being 'tall and turreted, like some very fat lighthouse'. It seems to have been unlike any other building on the Furness system.

Another station in Barrow — Island Road — was opened in 1899, to serve the expanding shipbuilding works on Barrow Island, where the workforce had now increased to 7,000. This two-platform structure was reached by a spur from the Ramsden Dock line, and was built on what was, in effect, a Barrow Island loop line, running from Shipyard Junction to Walney Ferry signalbox and making several connections into the shipyard.

Further investment was made in new freight rolling stock, with a large order in 1906 for 100 new 15-ton-capacity wagons, and in new paddle-steamers for the Fleetwood–Barrow service, but this coincided with yet another slump, particularly in the iron and steel industries, resulting in the FR dividend's declining from 7% in 1900 to 3% in 1906 and to no more than 1% in 1914 on the eve of World War 1.

During the whole of its existence, the Furness Railway had few accidents — indeed its proud boast was that no accident ever resulted in a passenger fatality — but perhaps the most serious was in the early morning of 28 February 1903, when, during a severe gale, the down Carnforth–Whitehaven mail train was blown onto its side when crossing the Leven viaduct. Fortunately, the train did not fall into the stormy waters of the estuary, and although 33 people were hurt, none of the injuries was serious.

For many years, the Furness had carried through coaches from other main-line railway companies, beginning with the Midland in 1867, and 1913 probably saw the zenith of this traffic. Four workings daily ran to and from the Furness line and London Euston, with other through coaches working to and from Manchester, Liverpool and Cambridge. Midland Railway carriages linked Leeds and

*Top left:* The decorative front cover of the January 1900 FR timetable. The vignettes include HMS *Niobe* docked at Barrow, and the steamer berth at Lake Side station.
*Cumbria Record Office, Kendal*

*Bottom left:* The January 1900 timetable listed the extensive through carriage workings to and from the Furness line. Note also the inclusion of services over the 3ft 0in-gauge Ravenglass & Eskdale Railway.
*Cumbria Record Office, Kendal*

*Top right:* Barrow (Island Road) station, probably taken in autumn 1964 at the time of gauging for Class 47s, an example of which is behind Class 5MT 4-6-0 No 45258. The building on the left is the signalbox; behind the locomotives a double-track layout continued, on a central reservation, towards the shipbuilding works.
*Ward Collection,*
*Cumbrian Railways Association*

*Centre right:* Almost certainly one of many six-wheel Thirds dating from the 1890s, this FR coach was still used on colliers' trains near Hednesford, Staffordshire, when photographed in June 1950. *O. H. Prosser*

*Bottom right:* Grange goods yard, looking towards Ulverston, c1910, showing the goods shed and a fine collection of FR vans and wagons. *L&GRP*

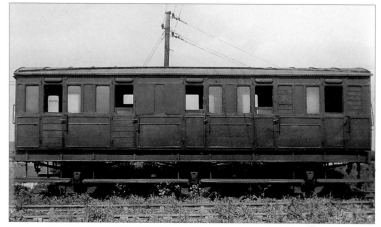

*Left:* Purchased by the FR in 1901 for Barrow–Fleetwood cross-bay services, the paddle-steamer *Lady Evelyn* was 200ft long, with a 24ft beam, and had a service speed of 17kt. The vessel was named after a member of the Cavendish family, from Holker Hall. After passing through several owners, she survived until May 1940 when she struck a wreck and sank in the English Channel while taking part in the Dunkirk evacuation. *Bucknall Collection / Ian Allan Library.*

*Above:* Built in 1905 and bought by the FR from the Barry Railway Co in 1910, the paddle-steamer *Lady Moyra* was 245ft long, with a beam of 29ft and a service speed of 17kt. The Barrow–Fleetwood service was withdrawn on the outbreak of war in 1914 and was never restored. Like the *Lady Evelyn*, the *Lady Moyra* was also sunk at Dunkirk, as the result of German bombing. *Bucknall Collection / Ian Allan Library*

*Left:* Just after the outbreak of World War 1, two FR 4-4-0s — No 33 built in 1896 and No 130 of 1913 — prepare to leave Barrow Central with a Carnforth train, conveying through London Euston coaches. The long-demolished Central South signalbox is visible behind the train locomotive, while Platform 4 — opened in May 1907 — can be seen in the background. *Bucknall Collection*

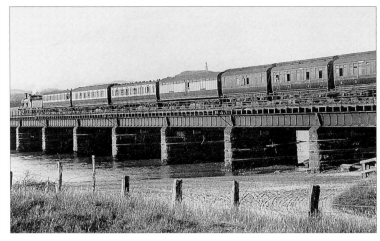

*Right:* Edwardian splendour on the Furness: an FR 4-4-0 of the 1901 build (numbered 126 to 129) crosses Eskmeals Viaduct, just south of Ravenglass, with what is almost certainly a Leeds–Whitehaven express. The first four vehicles of the train are Furness stock, while Midland vehicles (six-wheel Guard's Brake, six-wheel compartment Third and bogie composite Third/First) bring up the rear of the train. *Kerr Collection, Cumbrian Railways Association*

Bradford with Barrow, Lake Side and Whitehaven. These workings provided Furness and West Cumberland passengers with an excellent range of connections.

According to W. McGowan Gradon in *The Furness Railway: its Rise and Development, 1846-1923*, '…the Great War found the Furness Railway serving an area which was destined to play a big part in Great Britain's war effort', and the wartime arms drive brought a feverish boom to Barrow in particular, as well as better prospects to the railway. By 1915, buoyed up by increasing revenue, particularly from freight, the dividend was increased once more, to 2%. Part of this increase came from Sunday freight workings (previously largely unknown on the FR), mainly of coal traffic from the Lancashire coalfield to the fleet at Scapa Flow, which used the Cumberland Coast line because the main

Shap route was working at full capacity. Wartime demands also brought about the construction of a new branch line on the Cumberland coast, at Eskmeals, where Vickers, Sons & Maxim had opened a gun-testing range in 1897. Making a trailing connection to the down main line, the extensive private system allowed the movement of materials to and from Barrow, as well as within the high-security area, and was served by a new workmen's halt alongside the Furness junction. Further infrastructure work included the reconstruction of the Kent and Leven viaducts, in order to take heavier freight workings.

One casualty of the war was the surviving Belfast and Isle of Man services, which, together with the Fleetwood steamers, were withdrawn in 1914. Spasmodic sailings continued until 1936, when Ramsden Dock

*Right:* An unidentified LNWR 0-6-0 storms through Seascale station with a northbound freight, probably a coal train destined for Scapa Flow, during World War 1 (note the blackout paint on the station lamps). The edge of the commodious 'Refreshment Pavilion', built in 1913 and overlooking the Irish Sea, can just be seen to the right of the FR-pattern down side building. *Kerr Collection, Cumbrian Railways Association*

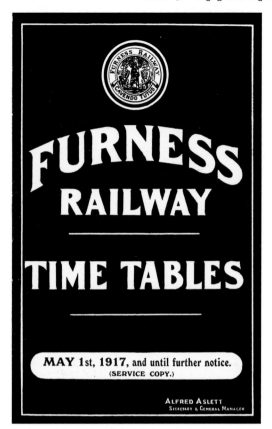

# FURNESS
## RAILWAY

---

## TIME TABLES

---

**MAY 1st, 1917, and until further notice.**
(SERVICE COPY.)

ALFRED ASLETT
SECRETARY & GENERAL MANAGER

*Left:* The Furness in wartime: cover of the May 1917 timetable. *Cumbria Record Office, Kendal*

*Below:* Eskmeals station in early BR days, looking north towards the River Esk viaduct. The Stationmaster's house once stood behind the shelter on the down side, but had been demolished by the time the photograph was taken. Eskmeals closed in 1959. *W. A. Camwell*

station was finally closed. Despite demolition of the station in 1938, the site continued to be known locally as 'the Belfast berth', and it is worth noting that, as late as the summer of 1970, a privately-organised sailing ran from this site on Barrow Island to the Isle of Man, using the 40-year-old turbine steamer *Lady of Mann*.

Towards the end of hostilities, F. J. Ramsden — the son of Sir James Ramsden — was appointed FR Chairman. As the railway company approached the end of its independent life, it seemed appropriate that the great families who had founded the company should still be running it at the end, for, in addition to Ramsden, Lord Richard Cavendish and the Duke of Devonshire were amongst the Board members. Alfred Aslett himself retired in 1918, aged 71, after nearly a quarter of a

century's service. David Joy, in *Cumbrian Coast Railways*, paid eloquent tribute to Aslett's career, writing that '…[after] the war years…he left behind a system…more capable of withstanding the looming [economic] crisis than the hotch-potch of [West Cumberland] routes'.

Aslett was succeeded as Company Secretary by his assistant, George Linton, who was an authority on the history and development of the FR, contributing several historical articles to the *Furness Railway Magazine* between 1921 and 1923.

In 1919 — the first full year of peace — freight traffic understandably slumped (to around 3 million tons, down from just under 5 million in 1916), but the vogue for tourism, stimulated by the lifting of wartime travel restrictions, resulted in more than 5 million passengers' being carried on Furness metals. However, in common with many other railway companies, the exigencies of war had made many demands on the company's resources, as well as delaying capital exenditure in other areas, with the result that the dividend was again reduced in 1921, to 1%. By this time, however, the days of the Furness Railway as an independent concern were numbered, as the Railway Act of 1921 provided for the formation of a new London, Midland & Scottish Railway, into which the Furness was to be absorbed. There was now clearly no point in additional heavy capital expenditure, the Furness preferring to leave this to the larger LMS company, although one major investment was made in the building of a new steel bridge over the River Duddon at Foxfield, replacing the elegant cast-iron viaduct of 1872, which in turn had replaced the original W&FJR structure of 1850.

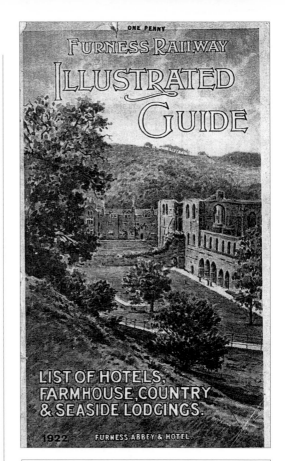

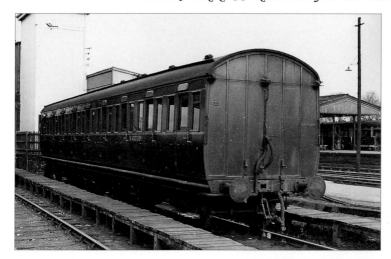

*Left:* In the 1950s, it was still possible to travel on British Railways in former Furness stock. A Third-class non-corridor coach built in 1920 stands at Gloucester as BR M15330 in 1950. Sister vehicle E15332M was observed at Shoeburyness, on the London, Tilbury & Southend system, as late as September 1956. *L&GRP*

*Centre left:* The junction station at Sellafield, seen here in LMS days, between the FR coastal route to Whitehaven, and the Whitehaven, Cleator & Egremont's inland line. The station buildings, similar to those at Haverthwaite, are adorned with LMS noticeboards, although the FR station nameboard remains on the extreme left of the building. *Ian Allan Library*

*Bottom left:* The large Furness Railway signalbox at Sellafield at the north end of the island platform, seen here in March 1969. The original FR 'Sellafield' sign is visible beneath the middle front window. *S. C. Dent*

*Right:* The Cleator Joint Lines and Cleator & Workington Railway tables from the May 1917 FR timetable. *Cumbria Record Office, Kendal*

*Below:* The end of the main line: the sharply-curved FR platforms at Whitehaven Bransty in BR days, with a DMU in the Carlisle bay on the left. The LNWR signalbox can be seen in the centre, and the pithead winding gear of a local colliery on the right. *P. J. Sharpe*

### CLEATOR JOINT LINES AND CONNECTIONS.

| DOWN. | 1 | 2 | 3 | 4 | 5 | 6 | 7 | 8 | 9 | 10 | 11 | 12 | 13 | 14 | 15 | 16 |
|---|---|---|---|---|---|---|---|---|---|---|---|---|---|---|---|---|
| | | | | | a.m. | | a.m. | | | | p.m. | | p.m. | | | |
| Carnforth .......depart | | | | | 4 55 | | 8 15 | | | | 1 40 | | 4 30 | | | |
| Grange-over-Sands,, | | | | | | | 8 40 | | | | 2 5 | | 4 55 | | | |
| Ulverston ,, | | | | | 5 27 | | 9 7 | | | | 2 32 | | 5 22 | | | |
| Barrow (Central) ,, | | | | | 5 53 | | 9 40 | | | | 3 5 | | 6 0 | | | |
| Millom ,, | | | | | 6 23 | | 1020 | | | | 3 45 | | 6 40 | | | |
| Seascale ,, | | | | | 6 35 | | 1057 | | | | 4 22 | | 7 13 | | | |
| Sellafield ...arrive | | | | | 6 38 | | 11 0 | | | | 4 25 | | 7 16 | | | |
| | | | | | a.m. | | a.m. | | p.m. | p.m. | | | | | | |
| Sellafield .......depart | | | | | | | 8 40 | | 1115 | | 5 20 | | 7 30 | | | |
| Beckermet .....arrive | | | | | | | 8 45 | | 1120 | | 5 25 | | 7 35 | | | |
| Egremont ,, | | | | | | | 8 53 | | 1128 | 1 35 | 4 10 ...5 33 | | 7 43 | | | |
| Woodend ,, | | | | | | | 8 57 | | 1132 | 1 39 | 4 14 ...5 37 | | 7 47 | | | |
| Moor Row ,, | | | | | | | 9 1 | | 1136 | 1 43 | 4 18 ...5 41 | | 7 51 | | | |
| | | a.m. | | | | | | | | | | | | | | |
| Moor Row .....depart | | 8 53 | | | | | 9 3 | | 1140 | 1 56 | 4 30 | | 7 52 | | | |
| White- (Corkickle arr. | | 9 0 | | | | | 9 11 | | 1148 | 2 5 | 4 38 | | 8 0 | | | |
| haven (Bransty ,, | | 9 5 | | | | | 9 16 | | 1153 | 2 10 | 4 45 | | 8 5 | | | |
| | a.m. | | a.m. | | a.m. | | p.m. | | | | p.m. | p.m. | | p.m. | | |
| White- (Bransty dep. | 6 15 | | 8 50 | | 10 30 | | 1240 | | | | 4 20 | 6 10 | | 8 20 | | |
| haven (Corkickle ,, | 6 18 | | 8 53 | | 10 33 | | 1243 | | | | 4 23 | 6 13 | | 8 23 | | |
| Moor Row ....arrive | 6 27 | | 9 2 | | 1q 43 | | 1252 | | | | 4 32 | 6 22 | | 8 32 | | |
| Moor Row .......depart | 6 25 | | 9 8 | | | | 1254 | | | | 4 35 | 5 50 | | 8 34 | | |
| Cleator Moor .. arrive | 6 33 | | 9 15 | | | | 1259 | | | | 4 40 | 5 55 | | 8 39 | | |
| Frizington ,, | 6 38 | | 9 20 | | | | 1 4 | | | | 4 45 | 6 | | 8 44 | | |
| Yeathouse ,, | 6 43 | | 9 25 | | | | 1 9 | | | | 4 50 | 6 5 | | 8 49 | | |
| Winder ,, | 6 47 | | 9 29 | | | | 1 13 | | | | 4 54 | 6 9 | | 8 53 | | |
| Rowrah ,, | 6 51 | | 9 33 | | | | 1 16 | | | | 4 58 | 6 12 | | 8 56 | | |
| Lamplugh ,, | 6 57 | | 9 39 | | | | | | | | 5 4 | | | | | |
| Ullock ,, | 7 1 | | 9 43 | | | | | | | | 5 8 | | | | | |
| Branthwaite ,, | 7 3 | | 9 47 | | | | | | | | 5 12 | | | | | |
| Bridgefoot ,, | 7 13 | | 9 55 | | | | | | | | 5 20 | | | | | |
| Broughton Cross ,, | 8 37 | | 1120 | | | | | | | | 5 40 | | | | | |
| Brigham ,, | 8 40 | | 1123 | | | | | | | | 5 43 | | | | | |

### CLEATOR & WORKINGTON RAILWAY, AND CONNECTIONS.

| DOWN. | 1 | 2 | 3 | 4 | 5 | 6 | 7 | 8 | 9 | 10 |
|---|---|---|---|---|---|---|---|---|---|---|
| | | | a.m. | | a.m. | | | | | |
| Carnforth............depart | | | 4 55 | | 8 15 | | | | | |
| Grange-over-Sands ...... ,, | | | | | 8 40 | | | | | |
| Ulverston ,, | | | 5 27 | | 9 7 | | | | | |
| Barrow (Central)........ ,, | | | 5 53 | | 9 40 | | | | | |
| Millom ,, | | | 6 23 | | 10 20 | | | | | |
| Seascale ,, | | | 6 35 | | 10 57 | | | | | |
| Sellafield ,, | | | 6 40 | | 11 15 | | | | | |
| Moor Row............arrive | | | 9 1 | | 11 36 | | | | | |
| | a.m. | | a.m. | | a.m. | | p.m. | | | |
| Moor Row Junction........depart | 7 40 | | 10 3 | | 1 5 | | 5 0 | | | |
| Cleator Moor ,, | 7 44 | | 10 7 | | 1 9 | | 5 4 | | | |
| Moresby Parks ,, | 7 51 | | 10 14 | | 1 16 | | 5 11 | | | |
| Distington ,, | 7 59 | | 10 22 | | 1 24 | | 5 19 | | | |
| High Harrington ,, | 8 3 | | 10 26 | | 1 28 | | 5 23 | | | |
| Workington (Central) ,, | 8 10 | | 10 33 | | 1 35 | | 5 30 | | | |
| Siddick Junction .....arrive | 8 14 | | 10 37 | | 1 39 | | 5 35 | | | |

Right to the end, the type of freight traffic which had justified the opening of the line in 1846 still existed. Despite the increased use of imported Spanish haematite, local ore was still being tripped from the Lindal and Dalton areas to the ironworks at Barrow and Ulverston, while Millom Ironworks continued to complement its Hodbarrow ore with output from the Cleator area. All three sites continued to take coke from the Durham coalfield, this traffic still taking the traditional route via Stainmore, Tebay and the Hincaster–Arnside line, and to despatch their finished products to the south and the east via the yards at Carnforth. Barrow Docks continued to generate large quantities of goods and general-merchandise traffic. The steep gradients and

*Above:* The FR platforms, complete with LNWR-style nameboards and signals, in September 1954. Class 5MT 4-6-0 No 45019 leaves with a Workington-bound train from the south, while Class 2P 4-4-0 No 40694 waits with a later departure in the Carlisle bay. *Ian Allan Library*

*Left: Le Chemin de Fer de Furness*: possibly printed for the FR stand at the Franco-British Exhibition in Paris in 1908, a French-language version of the company's *Circular Tours*.
*Cumbria Record Office, Barrow*

sharp curves on both sides of Lindal Summit had always caused operating problems for freight traffic, right from the line's opening, and banking engines continued to operate from Plumpton Junction, Park South and Roose; indeed, this practice continued, through LMS and BR days, into the diesel era and the early 1970s.

The Furness Railway ceased to exist at midnight on 31 December 1922. At its final Annual General Meeting, held at the Furness Abbey Hotel on 20 February 1923, it recorded gross receipts (excluding exceptional items) of nearly £1 million and expenses of £839,000, with a final dividend of 2%. This financially-competent overall performance, however, included one very sobering statistic. Revenue for the under-used Barrow Docks was £112,286, against expenses of £110,575 — the activities of the FR's Lakeland steamers were twice as profitable! The 1923 Grouping saw the Furness incorporated into the Furness & West Cumberland section of the LMS, which also included all former LNWR lines in the area: the Cleator Joint line, the Cleator & Workington Junction Railway, the Maryport & Carlisle and a 5¼-mile section of the former Solway Junction (Caledonian Railway) route.

At the end, the Furness Railway owned more than 250 route miles, 136 locomotives and 953 buildings in the area. Despite generally serving the area well, and pioneering Lakeland tourism, it failed to develop Barrow Docks as a rival to Liverpool; the port continued to operate well below capacity, Cavendish Dock was never fully commissioned, and the Irish traffic was lost to Heysham Harbour. Industry within the Furness hinterland failed to develop substantially beyond iron and steel making and shipbuilding, with even the latter struggling to

survive through its early years. However, this great over-optimism in forecasting the extent of economic growth and development was not uncommon to Victorian capitalism. As Pollard and Marshall said, '...[the Furness] retained [the Cavendish family motto] *Cavendo Tutus* throughout its existence. It might have taken warning from its loose translation — 'Achievement through caution'.

*Below left:* Another French-language publication, this time published in June 1910 for two International Expositions: the Belgian-English in Brussels and the Anglo-Japanese in England. *Cumbria Record Office, Barrow*

*Below right:* A useful Furness Railway chronology, issued by the company's Publicity Department in April 1912. Some of the dates differ from those shown elsewhere in this book, and may not be entirely reliable. *Cumbria Record Office, Barrow*

FURNESS RAILWAY. GRATIS.

CHEMIN DE FER DE FURNESS.

LES CHARMANTS

# Lacs Anglais

GRASMERE.

## Voyages Circulaires à :: Itinéraires Fixes ::

PAR LE
CHEMIN DE FER DE FURNESS.

Barrow-in-Furness, *Juin, 1910*     **ALFRED ASLETT,** *Secrétaire et Directeur Général.*

Stalles de la Compagnie du Chemin de fer de Furness, Cour E, Galérie de l'Industrie, Exposition Internationale de Bruxelles, et Exposition Anglo-Japonaise, Shepherd's Bush, Londres (Nos. 30, 31, et 32 Engineering Section).

## Furness Railway.

### DATES OF OPENING·

#### MAIN LINE.

| Year. | | M. | C. |
|---|---|---|---|
| 1846 | Dalton to Kirkby | 6 | 69 |
| 1847 | Roose to Barrow, Old Passenger Station | 1 | 33 |
| 1848 | Kirkby to Broughton | 3 | 43 |
| 1849 | Ravenglass to Whitehaven | 16 | 61 |
| 1850 | Foxfield to Ravenglass | 17 | 45 |
| 1851 | Lindal to Dalton | 1 | 53 |
| 1854 | Ulverston to Lindal | 2 | 68 |
| 1857 | Carnforth to Ulverston | 19 | 35 |
| 1867 | Millwood Junction to Dalton Junction | 0 | 33 |
| 1873 | Barrow, Old Station, to Ormsgill Junction | 1 | 70 |
| 1881 | St. Luke's Junction to Barrow Docks | 1 | 42 |
| 1882 | Barrow and Park Loop (Salthouse to Park) | 5 | 41 |
| | | 79 | 33 |

#### BRANCH LINES.

| Year | | M. | C. |
|---|---|---|---|
| 1846 | Goldmire Junction to Piel Pier | 6 | 13 |
| 1859 | Broughton to Coniston | 8 | 67 |
| 1863 | Hawcoat Branch | 0 | 52 |
| 1865 | Millom to Hodbarrow | 1 | 49 |
| 1867 | Crooklands to Stainton | 1 | 56 |
| 1869 | Levens Junction to Greenodd Junction | 0 | 29 |
| 1869 | Ulverston to Lake Side | 9 | 38 |
| 1873 | Salthouse Junction to Stank | 1 | 74 |
| 1876 | Arnside to Hincaster (Kendal Branch) | 5 | 25 |
| 1882 | Oak Lea and Goldmire Junction | 0 | 31 |
| 1883 | Plumpton Junction to Bardsea (Priory Station) | 2 | 0 |
| 1901 | Loco. Junction to Ramsden Dock (South Side) | 1 | 9 |
| 1906 | Cavendish Bridge Junction to Pulp Works Sidings | 1 | 6 |
| | | 40 | 49 |

#### JOINT LINES.

| Year | | M. | C. |
|---|---|---|---|
| 1855—1879. | L. & N.W. and Furness Joint Line | 34 | 24 |
| 1867 | (F. & M. Joint) Carnforth to Wennington | 9 | 50 |
| 1880 | Carnforth, F. & M. Curve | 0 | 21 |
| | | 44 | 15 |
| | Total | 164 | 17 |

#### STEAMERS.

|  | |
|---|---|
| 1859 | Coniston Steam Yachts |
| 1871 | Windermere Steam Yachts |
| 1901 | Barrow to Fleetwood Steamers |

| | |
|---|---|
| 1846 | Furness Abbey Hotel. |
| 1910 | George Romney's Early Home (1742—1755) Barrow-in-Furness. |

*General Manager's Office, Barrow-in-Furness, July, 1912,*

# 7. The Branches

The Furness main line had a number of branches, some of which were freight only, thus reflecting the company's main business. This short review gives an account of a selection of these lines.

### Arnside–Hincaster

A short section on this 5-mile 26-chain line, linking the FR at Arnside with the London & North Western Railway at Hincaster Junction, is included in Chapter 4. While its main purpose was to carry the heavy coke traffic from Durham to the Barrow area, without reversal in the Carnforth goods yards, the Furness also had running powers over the branch and on to Kendal, situated on the Windermere branch. This service originated at Grange-over-Sands, and the April 1910 timetable showed five weekday trains in each direction, taking 35 minutes for the 14¼ miles. On the branch proper, there were two intermediate stations, at Sandside and at Heversham, where the local grammar school was an important source of traffic.

*Left:* Arnside's up side building — an unattractive 1914 replacement of a wooden structure — is framed by the lattice footbridge. The goods yard, reached from the Hincaster branch, was behind the up platform, at a lower level. *Ian Allan Library*

*Below left:* Arnside signalbox, controlling the Hincaster branch junction, on 2 August 1968. Local building materials — limestone and red sandstone — were used in its construction. *J. Scrace*

*Right:* The newly-opened Newby Bridge Motor Car Platform in 1905. The following year, following replacement of the railmotor with locomotive-hauled stock, the platform was lengthened and the name changed to 'Newby Bridge Platform'. *L&GRP*

*Below right:* An interesting view of Lake Side station in the early 1900s. The pitched-roofed building to the right of the signal is the water-tower, adjoining which is the combined engine and goods shed. The signal post is painted green to harmonise with its surroundings — a practice adopted by the FR at several tourist stations. *L&GRP*

Passenger services over this line were suspended in May 1942, being permanently withdrawn in March 1953. Excursions, however, continued to use the line for several years after this date, especially those organised by the local Barrow paper — the *North Western Evening Mail* — to Scottish destinations such as the Trossachs or the Kyles of Bute. After withdrawal of the Durham coke trains, the line was closed north of Sandside Quarry in September 1963, with total closure coming in January 1972.

The branch was last used in May 1971, when the Royal Train was stabled overnight in the Hincaster platform at Arnside, *en route* to Barrow, where HM The Queen was to launch a nuclear submarine.

**Ulverston–Lake Side**
Running 9 miles 40 chains from Ulverston to Windermere (Lake Side) — the actual junction was at Plumpton — this picturesque line, alongside the Crake Estuary and up the Leven Valley, was opened throughout on 1 June 1869. The influence of the Midland Railway seems to have played a part in its promotion, since the decision to build as far as Newby Bridge (the

*Left:* A 1960s view of the 1938-built MV *Swan* on the Lakeside slipway, undergoing its winter overhaul. The vessel was constructed by Vickers-Armstrong in Barrow and transported in sections to Lakeside by rail for final assembly.
*British Transport Commission*

*Centre left:* Haverthwaite station, looking towards Lakeside, in 1947, the year after final closure to passengers. The main station building is a 'standard' FR design from the Lancaster architects Paley & Austin, and FR platform lamps are still in evidence. *L&GRP*

*Bottom left:* In summer 1955, Class 4F 0-6-0 No 44505 marshals a fine collection of pre-Nationalisation stock at Lakeside. *N. R. Knight*

*Right:* On 19 August 1959, Class 4MT 2-6-4T No 42589 stands at Lakeside with an Ulverston local. By this time, the engine shed door had been bricked up. Lake Windermere can be seen on the right. *R. E. Toop*

*Below right:* An FR signalling survivor on the Lakeside & Haverthwaite Railway: the lattice-post Haverthwaite up distant, photographed on 9 May 2000. Now fixed, this signal was formerly operational until BR closure of the branch on 6 September 1965, though for many years the arm had been an upper quadrant. *H. I. Quayle*

initial terminus) was taken by the Furness Railway at a meeting held at the Midland Hotel in Derby in October 1865, shortly before the opening of the F&M Joint line. Further evidence of MR involvement was the decision, at the same meeting, to build a curve at Leven Junction (near the main-line Leven viaduct), allowing through-running onto the branch from Carnforth, without reversal at Ulverston.

Although freight traffic was generated by Backbarrow Ironworks (where, remarkably, the furnace was in operation from 1711 until 1967) and by local gunpowder factories, the line's main *raison d'être* was tourist traffic to and from the commodious terminus at Lake Side, which O. S. Nock described as '...a miniature edition of Fishguard Harbour or Parkeston Quay, with space for three steamers to berth simultaneously...and a [high-level] refreshment pavilion giving fine views up the lake: [this was] a fully-fledged restaurant, where an orchestra held forth during...luncheon and tea'.

The Furness built, in 1904, a luxurious steam railcar, with observation windows, for the Lake Side services, together with a four-wheeled trailer, but increasing traffic in the 1905 season forced its replacement by conventional rolling stock, and the railcar was transferred to the Coniston branch. Two of these units were eventually built, and were the only engines ever to be constructed in the FR's Barrow works.

The April 1910 timetable showed a weekday service of six trains each way between Ulverston and the Lake Side terminus, taking 25 minutes for the trip, and this had increased to eight just before the Grouping, with one Carnforth–Lake Side working being routed via the Leven Curve. However, the line was primarily a tourist route,

*Left:* More than 80 years after passenger services were withdrawn, Conishead Priory station, photographed on 10 May 2000, survives (albeit extended and modernised) as a holiday home, complete with station clock. The occupants can be seen walking along the platform edge.
*H. I. Quayle*

with little traffic being generated by the intermediate stations of Greenodd and Haverthwaite, and in September 1938 the all-year-round passenger service was withdrawn. Summer services were operated in 1939, 1940, and (to a lesser extent) in 1941, but were not then reinstated until the summer of 1946.

This pattern of operation continued for the next 20 years until September 1965, when the passenger service was finally withdrawn. Part of the line, between Haverthwaite and Lake Side, remains open today as the Lakeside & Haverthwaite Railway, services having recommenced in May 1973.

### Ulverston–Conishead Priory

As mentioned in Chapter 5, the so-called Bardsea branch from Plumpton Junction was intended to be the first stage of a new line to Barrow, eliminating the steep banks each side of Lindal Summit. The initial impetus for construction came with the opening of Ulverston Ironworks in 1874, but, despite the contruction of earthworks, including a bridge, as far as Red Lane (near Bardsea), rails were only ever laid as far as Conishead Priory station, opened in June 1883. An intermediate halt, mainly to serve south Ulverston and the ironworks, was opened in June 1888.

*Left:* A Derby-built DMU enters Dalton's commodious station on a Barrow-bound working in the 1960s. Between the down platform and the stone wall ran the goods loop from Crooklands, which also gave access to the Stainton Quarry branch.
*Ward Collection,*
*Cumbrian Railways Association*

*Right:* Although most of the Stank branch — intended as part of a new Barrow–Lindal through route — was dismantled shortly after closure in 1901, the course of the line can still be followed today. As the line runs past Old Holbeck, on the climb to Stank, the earthworks are shown running from the left to the abutments of a bridge, whose decking has long since been removed. Photographed on 10 May 2000. *H. I. Quayle*

Passenger traffic for this roundabout four-mile route (all trains had to reverse at Plumpton Junction) was never very heavy, and the service was quickly reduced to one return working each day, leaving Ulverston at 11.55 and returning from Conishead Priory at 12.13, thereby making the service all but useless. This residual working was withdrawn on 1 January 1917, but most of the line remained intact for many years, and is believed to have seen irregular excursions until the 1930s. The section towards North Lonsdale Crossing is still extant (albeit out of use) at the time of writing, having been used by ironworks traffic until 1938, and then by the Glaxo plant until 1994. South of the crossing, the track remained in place as far as Priory Crossing, just before the terminus, until the mid-1960s, having been used for many years to store mothballed freight wagons.

Perhaps because of its relative isolation, Conishead Priory station has survived over 80 years of closure, and today, much extended, is in use as a holiday home.

### Stainton Quarry
This mineral-only line opened in 1868, to transport limestone from Stainton quarries to Barrow Ironworks. One mile 56 chains long, the steeply-graded branch was carrying more than 100,000 tons of the material each year, until closure in the mid-1960s.

The junction with the main line was at Crooklands, just northeast of Dalton. Removal of the box here by the LMS meant that access to

the branch was obtained by a headshunt at the end of an independent line from Dalton station, resulting in all trains' being propelled up the fierce gradient.

### Salthouse Junction–Stank
Mentioned briefly in Chapter 5, the two-mile mineral branch from Salthouse Junction was opened in 1873, serving the Barrow Haematite Co's Stank mine at a time when the price of haematite ore was doubling annually. As part of the proposed new line to Lindal from Salthouse, the earthworks were built for double track, but only a single line was ever laid.

The ore deposits at Stank were never as great as at Lindal or Park, and by the early 1900s were virtually exhausted. A search for coal deposits in the area could have provided additional traffic, but no traces were found, and the line was truncated to a long siding, terminating just west of the present A5087 at Roose, where occasional traffic was provided by the neighbouring sand quarry until the early 1960s.

Much of the route is still traceable today, with several bridge abutments remaining, the largest on the approach to the site of Stank mine.

### Barrow–Piel
This original section of the Furness Railway has been well covered in previous chapters. After the transfer of steamer services to Ramsden Dock in 1881, the direct line between Roose and Parrack Hall was taken out of use, resulting in a

2-mile 73-chain-long branch served from Salthouse Junction by a curve opened in 1873.

Initially, the line had one intermediate station, at Rampside, but a halt was opened on the branch, just beyond Salthouse Junction, in May 1920, probably to serve workmen at the adjacent gasworks which had opened three years earlier. The number of workings varied between four and five trains each way (plus some additional Saturday workings), taking 12 minutes for the 4 miles 25 chains between Barrow and Piel.

The passenger service was withdrawn on 6 July 1936, although a short section was left intact, giving access to the gasworks and pulpworks sidings, as well as making a connection with a line running along the south side of Cavendish Dock. In 1954, the opening of Barrow Power Station resulted in a short extension to this 'long siding', with final closure not coming until the mid-1980s.

## Hawcoat Quarry

This short branch, from Ormsgill Junction and less than one mile long, was opened in 1864 to serve the sandstone quarry which was to provide the lining walls for the new Devonshire Dock. It is not clear when this line was closed, but it was still in use in 1881, when new flats in the Hindpool area of Barrow were under construction. The line must have included some tight curves, as FR regulations prohibited six-coupled locomotives from working over the branch.

## Kirkby Slate Quarries

Reference is made in Chapter 2 to the importance of the Kirkby slate quarries traffic in supporting proposals for the Furness Railway.

The quarries themselves were situated nearly 800ft above sea level, and a 3ft 2¼in-gauge gravity-worked incline, one mile long and known as the 'Long Incline', was constructed to link the exchange sidings at Incline Foot with the quarry terminus at Wiseman's House, 460ft above sea level. Even this was not the highest point on the quarry system, rails reaching a height of 800ft at the slate sheds on Lady Rachel Hill.

The incline was constructed around 1840, and was in continuous operation until closure in 1952. Normal operation saw five full descending wagons pulling up five empty wagons. Track-lifting took place in 1954, and the line's most famous landmark — Sound Bridge, across the A595 road at Kirkby — was demolished in 1958.

The standard-gauge link to the main line (in reality, a section of the original FR) survived, out of use, for several years after closure of the incline.

## Foxfield–Coniston

Arguably the most scenic of the Furness Railway's branches, the 8-mile 67-chain Broughton-in-Furness-Coniston line was opened on 18 June 1859, the FR's extension from Kirkby to Broughton having opened 11 years earlier.

*Above:* In the mid-1960s, a pair of Derby-built DMUs stand under Foxfield's slate trainshed with a northbound Cumbrian coast working. Despite closure of the Coniston branch in 1958, the interior of the waiting building on the right continued to display a 'Change Here for the Coniston Branch' sign until demolition in 1969. *Ward Collection, Cumbrian Railways Association*

*Below left:* Taken around 1908, the steam railmotor and its trailers have just arrived at Foxfield from Coniston; passengers are awaiting a connecting service to Barrow and the south. *LPC*

Nominally independent, the Coniston Railway Co was supplied with motive power and rolling stock by the FR, and the Duke of Devonshire and James Ramsden sat on its board. The two companies were amalgamated in 1862. The line's main role, at least in its early days, was to transport copper ore from the Coniston mines, which had previously been moved by barge along Coniston Water, to be shipped by sea from the port of Greenodd.

Starting at 1 in 49 from the platform ends at Broughton, the branch climbed continuously, through the intermediate stations of Woodland and Torver, to the Furness Railway's highest summit, 345ft above sea level, from which it ran high above the lake to Coniston station. This was not, in fact, a true terminus, since the line continued for around half a mile, to the

so-called 'Copper House' — the trans-shipment point for crushed ore from the mines.

By the 1870s, the ore deposits were reaching exhaustion, and the railway became increasingly dependent on tourist traffic, the previously-mentioned steam yacht *Gondola* of 1859 being complemented by the *Lady of the Lake* in 1908; both vessels continued in service until 1939, when regular sailings ceased.

While the level of services was surprisingly high for a mountain branch — six return workings in 1882, rising to seven in 1922, and taking 25 minutes for the full 9½ miles — the line never attracted much excursion traffic, suffering from the distance between terminus and lake, as well as being too far from the major Lancashire and Yorkshire population centres.

*Above:* Looking south from Coniston station footbridge. FR signalling still controls the layout, while the single-road engine shed, with turntable just visible behind, can be seen on the left. Little freight traffic is in evidence. *L&GRP*

*Below:* Torver station, photographed on 31 July 1954. The passing-loop here was removed in 1897. The building still survives today, as a private dwelling. *W. A. Camwell*

*Above:* Not long before closure in October 1958, push-pull-fitted Class 2MT 2-6-2T No 41217 stands under Coniston's overall roof with an auto-train from Foxfield. One of the notices on the right is advertising Lake Windermere steamer sailings. *R. E. Toop*

Closure to passenger traffic came on 6 October 1958, a freight service lingering on until 30 April 1962. Despite a reopening campaign, based on the inadequacy of the Coniston–Foxfield road for the replacement bus service, the track was lifted in the spring of 1963. Although the station buildings at Broughton, Woodland and Torver remain in private use, Coniston's magnificent terminus was allowed to decay, and, despite a plan to develop apartments within the structure, demolition took place in 1968.

### The Ravenglass–Murthwaite Branch

The Ravenglass & Eskdale Railway is well known as a 15in-gauge tourist line, running 7 miles to a terminus at Boot in the upper reaches of the Esk Valley, but the existence of a 2½-mile standard-gauge line, straddling the narrow-gauge route, is perhaps less well known.

The branch's origins lay in the 1927 rebuilding of the Murthwaite stone-crushing plant, the output of which, having reached Ravenglass over 15in-gauge metals, was then trans-shipped into standard-gauge wagons. To avoid the trans-shipment problem, the R&E management decided to build a new standard-gauge line from Murthwaite to exchange sidings in Ravenglass goods yard; for space reasons in the hilly countryside, the new line could not be laid alongside the existing route, and the narrow gauge was therefore gauntletted between the standard gauge. The line was completed on 21 November 1929, marking the end of the narrow-gauge ballast traffic between the crushing plant and Ravenglass. Motive power was provided by a chain-driven Kerr, Stuart 0-6-0 diesel.

Although disused after the cessation of stone traffic in 1953, the standard-gauge line survived until around 1964, when the connection to the exchange sidings in Ravenglass was severed upon closure of Ravenglass goods yard.

*Above:* Probably in the last years of the 19th century, an unidentified FR 0-6-0 is pictured with an up freight in Coniston's Platform 3. The signalbox, which was originally at Carnforth Junction (F&M), was re-erected here in 1896, and looks relatively new. *Bucknall Collection*

*Below:* In April 1947, ex-LNWR Class 1P 2-4-2T No 6718 stands outside Coniston's slate-built engine shed. This locomotive class dated from 1890. *R. Roberts*

*Above:* A 1908 view of Ravenglass goods yard. Two FR cattle-trucks stand to the right of the goods shed, whilst, in the centre, several loaded stone-wagons stand adjacent to the trans-shipment gantries. In the background, 3ft 0in-gauge Ravenglass & Eskdale Railway 0-6-0T *Devon* blows off outside the original R&E station, in front of which two narrow-gauge wagons can also be seen. *L&GRP*

*Below:* On 23 July 1952, Class 3F 0-6-0 No 52418 collects stone traffic from Ravenglass yard; this would have been worked up from Murthwaite over the mixed-gauge section. Note the staggered platforms and the Furness Railway goods shed, in front of which stands what appears to be an ex-Midland Railway coach converted to engineers' use. *A. Newton*

# 8. Locomotives

## Furness Railway

The Furness Railway ordered its first locomotives, for use in the construction of the line, from the Liverpool company of Bury, Curtis & Kennedy, these being delivered in 1844 and numbered 1 and 2. These 0-4-0 tender locomotives were distinguished by their bar frames and haystack-shaped fireboxes, and in 1846 were joined by the nearly-identical Nos 3 and 4 , the former being the famous and long-preserved 'Coppernob'. A local story relates that James Ramsden, newly appointed

Locomotive Superintendent of the FR, accompanied these locomotives by sea from Liverpool to Barrow. With Ramsden taking an increasingly higher profile in the company's management, he quickly relinquished this post to Mr. R. Mason, during whose long tenure (to 1896) the company never designed its own locomotives, preferring standard designs from a single outside supplier.

By 1851 increasing ore traffic was requiring heavy rostering for the 'Burys', resulting in the purchase of two 2-2-2 well-tanks from Sharp

*Below:* FR 0-4-0 No 4, built in 1846 and identical to No 3, nicknamed 'Coppernob'. Water to the right of the tender suggests a Barrow Docks location. Withdrawal took place in 1900. *Bucknall Collection / Ian Allan Library*

*Right:* The first of the Fairbairns: FR 0-4-0 No 7, delivered in 1854. Note the closed splashers over the wheels, when compared to the Bury locomotives.
*Bucknall Collection / Ian Allan Library*

*Centre right:* FR 0-4-0 No 9 outside the old Barrow Town station in St George's Square. The date is around 1886/7, as the lantern tower of Barrow Town Hall, seen to the right of the signal, is still under construction. The locomotive was withdrawn in 1901.
*Bucknall Collection / LPC*

*Below:* FR 2-2-2WT No 22 stands at Foxfield in 1886 on a Coniston–Barrow working. From their uniforms, it appears that all Foxfield station staff are on the platform. The Stationmaster's house, seen above the train's rear coach, still exists today.
*Bucknall Collection / Ian Allan Library*

Bros of Manchester, mainly for use on passenger services; these were numbered 5 and 6. The freight locomotive fleet was further augmented in 1854 and 1855 by the purchase of four additional Bury-type locomotives — Nos 7 to 10 — although these were built by

W. Fairbairn of Manchester, the Liverpool company having ceased trading. These were slightly larger than Nos 1 to 4.

The opening of the Ulverston & Lancaster Railway in 1857 increased substantially the route mileage worked by the FR, as a result of

*Left:* FR 2-2-2WT No 36, built by Sharp, Stewart in 1886, photographed in the Coniston platform at Foxfield. Note the unusual two-piece cab on this locomotive, and what appears to be a single-line tablet holder on the bunker rim. The water-tower and the Prince of Wales public house (behind the locomotive) still exist today. *Bucknall Collection / Ian Allan Library*

*Bottom left:* A works photograph of FR 2-2-2WT No 35. The lining on the bunker is not the Furness pattern, and the full cab roof has yet to be fitted. The locomotive was withdrawn from capital stock in 1896. *Bucknall Collection / Ian Allan Library.*

*Above:* FR 0-4-0 No 14, photographed in May 1876 at Ravenglass. The Furness Railway number plate, on the boiler side, appears to be of a non-standard design; the maker's plate is on the cabside. *Bucknall Collection / Ian Allan Library*

*Below:* FR 0-4-0 No 16 shunting Barrow yard, sometime after the closure of Barrow Town (in the background) in 1882. Note the deeper splashers. The church behind the locomotive is St George's, consecrated in 1861 — the year in which the locomotive was delivered. *L&GRP*

which two additional well-tanks, numbered 11 and 12, and almost identical to Nos 5 and 6, were purchased from Sharp Bros. These locomotives proved both reliable and economical, with the result that the Furness purchased an additional two — Nos 21 and 22 — in 1864, with four more following as Nos 34 to 37 in 1866. Larger cylinders and boilers distinguished these from the earlier well-tanks.

In 1858 W. Fairbairn delivered an additional two 0-4-0 tender locomotives — Nos 13 and 14 — followed by Nos 15 and 16 in 1861. Shortly

afterwards, Fairbairn ceased trading, and the next batch of 0-4-0 tender locomotives was delivered by Sharp, Stewart & Co — the successors to Sharp Bros. Delivered between 1863 and 1866, and numbered 17 to 20 and 25 to 28, these locomotives differed considerably in appearance from the earlier tender locomotives, having plate frames and a more conventional round-topped firebox. Six of these locomotives were sold between 1870 and 1873 to the Barrow Haematite Steel Co, which had them rebuilt as saddle-tanks. Almost 100 years later, in 1960,

*Above:* The last class of FR 0-4-0s: No 27, built in 1866 by Sharp, Stewart & Co. No 20 of the same class is now preserved on the Lakeside & Haverthwaite Railway. *LPC*

*Above:* FR 0-4-0 No 28, photographed near Barrow goods depot. While six locomotives of this class were sold to the Barrow Haematite Steel Co, Nos 27 and 28 remained FR locomotives, not being taken out of service until 1918. *Bucknall Collection / Ian Allan Library*

*Above:* FR 0-4-0ST No 95, built in 1874 and photographed in the Barrow area. The main duties of this class were shunting the dockside lines and working the local mineral branches. *Bucknall Collection / Ian Allan Library*

*Below:* The first of the FR 0-6-0s: although carrying its post-1918 number (61), this locomotive was originally No 29, having been delivered new in 1866. When new, no cab was fitted, only a front weatherboard. *Cumbria Record Office, Barrow*

*Above:* Displaying a Class 1 headcode, FR 0-6-0 No 85, built in 1873, stands at Kents Bank around the start of the 20th century. The rear coach, of Midland design, is a through working from Barrow to Leeds. Note the effects of two Pettigrew-era changes: the relocation of the number plate from boiler side to cabside, and the letters 'FR' on the tender. *Bucknall Collection / Ian Allan Library*

*Below:* In its original condition, before the fitting of vacuum brakes, FR 0-6-0 No 93 stands at Barrow. Note the Great Northern Railway-type cab. *Bucknall Collection / LPC*

*Above:* FR 0-6-0 No 55 photographed after 1896, with number plate moved to the cabside. The tender does not display the 'FR' initials, nor the usual pattern of curved rivets. *Bucknall Collection / LPC*

*Above:* A fine shot of FR 0-6-0 No 50, delivered in 1883 as one of the last members of a class first introduced in 1866. The location is probably Lake Side. *Bucknall Collection / Ian Allan Library*

two of these locomotives — Nos 20 and 25 — survived into static preservation in the grounds of two local schools; No 20 has been restored to its original 1863 condition, and, now Britain's oldest operating standard-gauge steam locomotive, is based on the Lakeside & Haverthwaite Railway.

For shunting at Barrow Docks, Sharp, Stewart supplied two 0-4-0 saddle-tanks — Nos 23 and 24 — in 1864. Four slightly modified locomotives from the same supplier — Nos 94 to 97 — were delivered in 1874.

With the increasing weight of mineral trains over the steep gradients each side of Lindal Summit, the FR needed more powerful locomotives, and once again turned to Sharp, Stewart's catalogue. The result was an 0-6-0 tender locomotive, of which no fewer than 55 — the largest of the FR classes — were built between 1866 and 1884. Relatively small but very economical and reliable, the first nine of

the so-called 'Sharpies' were numbered 29 to 33 and 38 to 41. Whilst the basic design remained unchanged throughout the production run, pre-1873 locomotives had only a weatherboard for protection against the elements, whilst the later versions had a cab. When W. F. Pettigrew was appointed Locomotive Superintendent in 1896, these useful locomotives were modernised with vacuum brakes and steam heating for use on passenger trains, as well as with new boilers, and 27 — nearly half the class — survived into LMS ownership in 1923. One of this class — No 115 — was lost in the well-known Lindal subsidence of 1892, and now lies several hundred feet below the present main line.

Banking of freights over Lindal Summit — from Plumpton Junction and from Park South — had also been common practice for many years, and, to complement the heavier train locomotives, the FR ordered new 0-6-0 side-tanks from Sharp, Stewart, the first — Nos

*Below:* With a Furness station lamp-post in the foreground, FR 0-6-0 No 18 — one of the early members of the class — stands at Lake Side in 1895. *L&GRP*

*Right:* Well away from its original haunts, FR 0-6-0 No 92 stands with a miners' train at Buckhill Colliery, on the northernmost section of the Cleator & Workington Junction Railway, probably around the time of World War 1. *Kerr Collection, Cumbrian Railways Association*

*Below:* FR 0-6-0 No 115, renumbered from No 114 in 1898 and shown as rebuilt with new boiler and cab in 1910, giving the locomotive a more up-to-date appearance, although the original tender was retained. The original No 115 was lost in the 1892 Lindal subsidence. Behind can be seen one of the FR's 4-4-0s, introduced in 1896 for express workings. *Bucknall Collection / Ian Allan Library*

*Bottom:* FR 0-6-0 No 63, with 'FR' initials on the tender. *Bucknall Collection / Ian Allan Library*

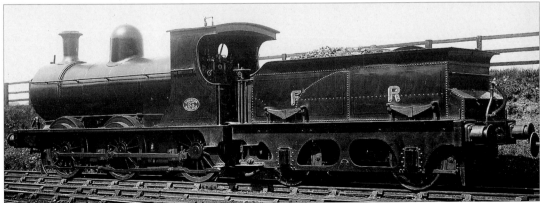

*Above:* No 30 was the second of the FR 0-6-0s, delivered in 1866 and later re-boilered. This photograph, probably taken at Moor Row around 1920, shows a tender weatherboard, fitted as additional protection from the elements on the exposed West Cumberland lines. *Cumbria Record Office, Barrow*

*Below:* Probably taken not long after delivery in 1873, FR 0-6-0T No 82 and crew stand outside Barrow's station in St George's Square. These locomotives were nicknamed 'Neddies'. Note the long side tanks, with hole to allow access to the motion. *LPC*

*Above:* FR 0-6-0T No 83 stands at Moor Row shed not long before the 1923 Grouping. The cabside sheets were unofficial additions by the shed staff, since the unmodified cabs provided little protection from the elements. These locomotives were never fitted with vacuum brakes. *Bucknall Collection / Ian Allan Library*

*Above:* FR 2-4-0 No 58, in 'as-built' 1871 condition. These were passenger locomotives, identical to those in operation on the Cambrian Railways at the same time. This locomotive was never rebuilt, being withdrawn in 1918. *LPC*

*Above:* FR 2-4-0 No 71 and crew at Barrow. Built in 1871, this locomotive was rebuilt as a 2-4-2T in 1891. *L&GRP*

*Below:* A posed view of FR 2-4-0 No 44 in 1884, heading FR passenger stock in front of Barrow Central North signalbox. The present and much larger box on the same site was opened in September 1907. *Bucknall Collection / Ian Allan Library*

51 and 52 — being delivered in 1867. An additional four locomotives were delivered in 1872 and 1873 as Nos 68, 69, 82 and 83.

Increasing passenger traffic, necessitating longer trains, also required more powerful traction than the small 2-2-2 well-tanks, and in 1870 Sharp, Stewart supplied the first two of a new class of 2-4-0 tender locomotives — Nos 1 and 2 (the 1844 'Burys' which originally carried these numbers had been scrapped or sold out of service). These locomotives, eventually reaching 18 in number, became the FR's standard passenger class until around the turn of the century. The final two were delivered in 1882.

*Above:* The first member of the class — FR 2-4-0 No 1 — stands at Carnforth in the early years of the 20th century at the head of an up passenger train. FR passenger stock is stabled on the loop behind the locomotive, a down platform not being constructed until the 1930s. *L&GRP*

*Below:* FR 2-4-2T No 73, converted in 1891 from a 2-4-0 tender locomotive. This engine was withdrawn in 1919. *LPC / Bucknall Collection*

*Above:* FR 2-4-2T No 71, photographed after 1896, showing the letters 'FR' on the side tanks and the number plate on the bunker sides. Note also the addition of three guard-rails to the top of the bunker, to increase capacity. *Bucknall Collection / Ian Allan Library*

*Below:* FR 4-4-0 No 121, built by Sharp, Stewart in 1891, stands near the locomotive depot at Carnforth. This was the FR's first 4-4-0 class (nicknamed the 'Seagulls'), the primary duties of which were the Ramsden Dock boat trains. Note the bogie splashers, which were later removed. *L&GRP*

*Above:* Photographed at Barrow, FR 4-4-0 No 122 as originally built, with boiler-mounted number plates. The outside-framed six-wheel tender was an enlarged version of the old FR standard four-wheel design. *Bucknall Collection / Ian Allan Library.*

*Below:* FR 4-4-0 No 123 on Carnforth shed around the start of the 20th century. Note that the bogie splashers have now been removed. Carnforth Station Junction signalbox can be seen above the locomotive's buffer beam. *LPC*

*Above:* FR 4-4-0 No 36, built in 1896 by Sharp, Stewart to handle the most important passenger services. Note the more modern tender, with full-width body, than in previous designs. As with the previous 4-4-0s, the bogie splashers were soon removed. *LPC*

*Below:* FR 4-4-0 No 34 pulls into Ravenglass at the head of a southbound express of Furness stock. This locomotive was renumbered 46 in 1920, and was the first of the class to be withdrawn, in 1927. *Kerr Collection, Cumbrian Railways Association*

*Top right:* A classic Furness location: FR 4-4-0 No 37, in immaculate condition, heads a Barrow-bound train near Grange. *L&GRP / Bucknall Collection*

*Bottom right:* Around the start of the 20th century, FR 4-4-0 No 35 leaves Grange at the head of a 10-coach Morecambe–Lake Side express. The fifth vehicle is a Midland Railway clerestory coach, which may have worked through from West Yorkshire and been added at Carnforth. *Ian Allan Library*

In 1891, seven of the 1872 batch were rebuilt as 2-4-2 radial-tanks, mainly for use on the Lake Side branch and on Grange–Morecambe/Kendal services, although finally migrating to the Cleator area for use on the Joint Lines.

After 1881 and the opening of Ramsden Dock station, increasing Irish boat train traffic from the Midland Railway required something more powerful than the 2-4-0s, and once again the FR board turned to Sharp, Stewart. The manufacturer had already supplied the

Cambrian Railways with a 4-4-0 tender design, and the same type was ordered by the Furness, being delivered in 1891 as Nos 120 to 123. Nicknamed 'Seagulls', these locomotives were the first FR type with a six-wheeled tender, although continuing with the practice of outside springs above the running plate. A larger version of the class was introduced in 1896, with 6ft-diameter driving wheels and larger boilers; six (Nos 21, 22, and 34 to 37) were delivered in 1896, with an additional two (Nos 124 and 125)

*Top:* The first class of Pettigrew's standard goods locomotives: FR 0-6-0 No 14, built by Sharp, Stewart in 1899 and fitted with a Phoenix superheater. *Bucknall Collection / Ian Allan Library*

*Above:* With a Whitehaven–Carnforth express goods — one of the class's main duties — FR 0-6-0 No 7 (the first of the class) heads south through Ravenglass. Note the FR down starter on the left: the lamp was secured in the low-level position for daytime maintenance, before being winched up the post for night use. *Bucknall Collection / Ian Allan Library*

*Above:* FR 0-6-0 No 9 runs along the sea wall near Grange with coke empties from Barrow, destined for Tebay, from where they would be worked over the North Eastern Railway's Stainmore route to County Durham.
*Bucknall Collection / L&GRP*

in 1900, all surviving until well into LMS days. As an experiment, Nos 34 and 37 were fitted with superheaters in 1913, but the devices were removed the following year.

Following Mason's retirement in 1896, Furness motive power policy changed. The new Locomotive, Carriage & Wagon Superintendent, W. F. Pettigrew, came from the much larger London & South Western Railway, where he had been assistant to the renowned William Adams, and immediately began to work on his own standard designs (although much LSWR influence was prevalent). The first evidence of this came in 1898, with the introduction of a new class of 0-6-2 tank engine to work over the Cleator-district lines in West Cumberland. Numbered 112 to 114, these locomotives were also built by Sharp, Stewart, continuing the FR's relationship with this locomotive builder.

As well as designing locomotives, Pettigrew produced a standard book on the subject, *A Manual of Locomotive Engineering, with an Historical Introduction*, published in 1899 and now a collector's item.

Orders were also placed in 1898 for a new class of 0-6-0 freight locomotive, with boiler, cylinders, wheels and motion all interchangeable with those of the new Cleator tanks. Twelve locomotives — Nos 7 to 18 — were ordered, but for the first time in Furness locomotive history, two suppliers were chosen, half the class being supplied by Sharp, Stewart and half by Nasmyth, Wilson & Co of Patricroft, Manchester. Principal duties for these locomotives were the Durham coke trains, which they worked to and from Tebay, and Carnforth–Whitehaven freights, although the whole class was also fitted with vacuum brakes and steam heating for passenger working. All the class survived into LMS ownership, the last not being withdrawn until 1936.

With the continuing growth in passenger traffic over the Furness main line, Pettigrew designed a new class of 4-4-0 tender locomotives, based on the larger version of the 'Seagulls', and these were delivered between 1900 and 1901 as Nos 126 to 129. The builder was the North British Locomotive Co of

Glasgow, although the order had been placed with Sharp, Stewart, which by now had been absorbed by the Scottish company. With 6ft 6in driving wheels and 26in x 18in cylinders, these locomotives were larger than their predecessors, and handled all Carnforth–Whitehaven expresses for more than 12 years.

As mentioned earlier, in 1904 the FR built the first of two four-coupled railmotor cars, for use on the Lake Side branch. These were the

only engines ever built at the company's Barrow works.

Additional 0-6-2 tank locomotives, similar to the 1898 batch but with larger driving wheels, were introduced in 1904, five being supplied by the North British Locomotive Co (NBL) and five by Nasmyth, Wilson. These were versatile locomotives, being used on both passenger and freight workings, and one example — No 101 — almost survived until British

*Above:* A member of the first class of Pettigrew's 0-6-0 goods locomotives, No 12 (the last of the Nasmyth, Wilson batch) stands at Moor Row not long before the 1923 Grouping. *Cumbria Record Office, Barrow*

*Below:* FR 0-6-0 No 16 trundles into Carnforth with an up mixed freight in 1923, the year following the end of the Furness Railway's independent existence. The locomotive looks less spotless than in FR days. To the right of the locomotive, the FR's Carnforth goods yard can just be seen; this yard still survives today for engineers' trains. *Ian Allan Library*

*Above:* The first of a new class of FR 4-4-0s, No 126, with 6ft 6in driving wheels, nears journey's end and runs past the Furness freight yard at Carnforth with a Whitehaven–Carnforth express. The fifth and sixth vehicles appear to be LNWR stock, probably destined for London Euston. *L&GRP / Bucknall Collection*

*Below:* FR 4-4-0 No 128 stands outside Barrow's commodious depot. Note the three rails on the tender, which allowed a capacity of 5½ tons of coal. *Bucknall Collection / Ian Allan Library*

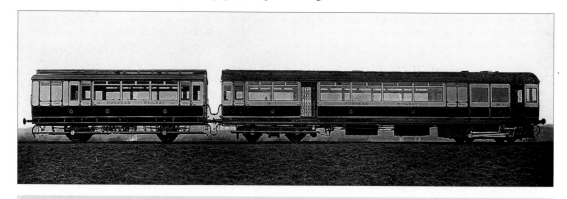

*Above:* FR steam railmotor car No 1, coupled to its dedicated 28-seat trailer. The trailer had its own driving compartment at the left-hand end. Note the steel lattice gate across the motor car's left-hand vestibule.
*Bucknall Collection / Ian Allan Library*

*Below:* Standing in Coniston's Platform 2, one of the FR's railmotor cars and trailers awaits its next turn of duty. The driving trailer is facing in the direction of the junction with the main line at Foxfield. *LPC*

*Above:* FR 0-6-2T No 98, the first of the class built in 1904, stands at the head of a Cleator & Workington Junction local: note the service indicator 'C&W 9' on the front left-hand lamp bracket. *Cumbria Record Office, Barrow*

*Below:* One of the North British Locomotive Co FR 0-6-2Ts, No 107, built in 1904. A Furness Railway crest has been applied to the leading splasher. With their 5ft 1in driving wheels, they were classified as mixed traffic locomotives. One engine, No 101, survived with the LMS until 1946.
*Bucknall Collection / H. Gordon Tidey / Ian Allan Library*

*Above:* FR 0-6-2T No 103 stands at Grange with a Barrow-bound stopping train, consisting entirely of Furness stock. *L&GRP / Bucknall Collection*

*Below:* On the final approach to the terminus at Lake Side, FR 0-6-2T No 103 arrives with a seven-vehicle local from Ulverston. The date is likely to be a summer after World War 1, as the last vehicle in the train is sporting the FR's post-1915 overall blue livery. *L&GRP*

*Above:* FR 0-6-2T No 97, built by the North British Locomotive Co in 1907, was almost identical to the previous 0-6-2T class, but had an extended bunker and shorter side tanks for better weight distribution. No 97 was the last of the class to be withdrawn, as LMS No 11636, in 1941. *Bucknall Collection / Ian Allan Library*

*Below:* The final development of the FR 0-6-2T: FR No 93, built by Kitson & Co in 1912, was one of four 'Improved Cleator Tanks', and spent most of its life in the Moor Row area, where its high tractive effort proved useful. The LMS scrapped this locomotive as early as 1929. *LPC / Bucknall Collection*

Railways days, not being withdrawn until 1946. Six almost identical examples were built by NBL in 1907, the only difference being better weight distribution, which gave them wider route availability. Between 1912 and 1914, four more were built, this time by Kitson & Co of Leeds, and were known as the 'Improved Cleator Tanks'; the main difference from the earlier batch was a larger boiler with higher pressure.

Further 0-6-0 tender locomotives, using components identical with the 1904 tank locomotives, were delivered by NBL in 1907, and were numbered 3 to 6. The class was divided between Carnforth and Whitehaven sheds, for express goods work and for seasonal excursion traffic.

Pettigrew now turned his attention to replacing the ageing shunting fleet, and in 1910 introduced a new class of 0-6-0 side-tanks, the

first six of which were delivered from the Vulcan Foundry at Newton-le-Willows and numbered 19 to 24 (later renumbered 55 to 60). Their main duties were shunting the dock lines and the marshalling yards in Barrow, but two of the class were later shedded at Moor Row for passenger duties on West Cumberland branch lines. In 1915, two more were delivered (51 and 52), this time from Kitson, with a further two (53 and 54) being delivered the following year from the Vulcan Foundry.

The development of the Furness 0-6-0 tender locomotive probably reached its zenith in 1913, with the introduction of the first four of a new class of powerful large-boilered locomotives with 4ft 7½in driving wheels. Delivered from NBL, they were mainly used on the heaviest iron-ore and coke workings, although they were also vacuum braked for use on passenger services. NBL delivered a further two in 1914, with Kitson and NBL each providing four more in 1918; the final five were delivered by NBL in 1920. The 19-strong class carried the numbers 1, 2, and 19 to 35. Some of the class survived until well into British Railways days, No 33 being withdrawn in August 1957 as BR No 52510.

*Left:* Still in works grey livery, FR 0-6-0T No 51, built by Kitson & Co of Leeds in 1915, although the first of the class dated from 1910. This was Pettigrew's standard locomotive class for shunting duties. This photograph appears to show the FR coat of arms between the letters on the side tank. After only 19 years' use, this locomotive was withdrawn in 1934. *LPC*

*Below left:* FR 0-6-0T No 56, renumbered from 20 in 1918, shunts a tank wagon at Carnforth, near the Furness yard, in 1923. This locomotive was built by the Vulcan Foundry at Newton-le-Willows. *L&GRP*

*Above:* The final development of the Furness 0-6-0 goods locomotive: a works' livery photograph of FR No 27, built in 1914 by the North British Locomotive Co. *Bucknall Collection / Ian Allan Library.*

*Below:* With a heavy Tebay–Barrow coke train of NER wagons, 1920-built FR 0-6-0 No 32, in immaculate condition, runs through the scenic Lune Gorge and over Dillicar water-troughs. *Bucknall Collection / Ian Allan Library*

Also seen in 1913 was the final development of the Furness 4-4-0, this passenger class using the same boiler as the 1913 0-6-0s. Numbered 130 to 133 and once again built by NBL, these powerful locomotives were used on the principal Furness line expresses to and from Lancaster, although, because of their weight, the Civil Engineer frowned on their use north of Barrow. Additional branch-line passenger motive power came two years later, in 1915, with the delivery of two 4-4-2 tank locomotives from Kitson & Co,

numbered 38 and 39; these were specifically designed for working branch-line services to Coniston, Lake Side and Kendal, although they were also used on workmen's services in the Barrow area. In 1916, the class increased to six, with the delivery of two locomotives from the Vulcan Foundry — Nos 40 and 41 — and two more from Kitson — Nos 42 and 43.

After nearly a quarter of a century as Locomotive Superintendent, Pettigrew retired in 1920 and was succeeded by D. L. Rutherford,

*Left:* As British Railways Class 3F 0-6-0 No 52509, ex-FR No 32 displays a new boiler and modified cab in this 1950s photograph. This locomotive was not scrapped until 1956. *Ian Allan Library*

*Below left:* The last survivor (apart from the 0-4-0STs still at work in Barrow Steelworks): ex-FR 0-6-0 No 33 is seen here in BR days as No 52510. Note the Fowler-pattern smokebox door. Considering that this view was taken not long before withdrawal in 1957, the locomotive is remarkably clean. *Ian Allan Library*

*Above:* Pettigrew's magnificent finale: the powerful FR 4-4-0s Nos 130 to 133 worked the Barrow–London Euston through trains as far as Lancaster, where LNWR motive power took over. No 132, pictured here, was built by the North British Locomotive Co in 1914. *LPC*

*Below:* FR 4-4-0 No 131 heads away from Carnforth with a Barrow-bound stopping train. Note the horsebox marshalled immediately behind the locomotive. Because of their weight, the Civil Engineer was not keen to see these locomotives used north of Barrow. Pettigrew, with his Eastleigh experience, may have been influenced by the London & South Western Railway's 'T6' class when designing the FR locomotives.
*Bucknall Collection / Ian Allan Library*

*Above:* A Kitson & Co works photograph: the first of the FR's handsome 4-4-2Ts, No 38, built in 1915. Equally at home on the Lake District branches or Barrow local services, they had a short life, the entire class being withdrawn by 1932. *LPC / Bucknall Collection*

*Below:* A view of FR 4-4-2T No 39 on Barrow shed, probably in early LMS days. The FR lining can still be seen, but the tanksides are devoid of 'FR' or 'LMS' lettering. *Bucknall Collection / Ian Allan Library*

who proceeded to introduce the last express locomotive design for the Furness Railway. This was a massive inside-cylindered 4-6-4 tank engine, larger than anything previously seen on the Furness system. Built by Kitson and nicknamed 'Jumbos', the first four locomotives — Nos 115 to 118 — were delivered late in 1920; the delivery of No 119, in January 1921, marked the end of an era in Furness locomotive design. These capable and powerful locomotives were used mainly on express and mail trains between Carnforth and Barrow, their bogies allowing the tight curves in the Barrow and Dalton areas to be easily negotiated.

*Above:* The last Furness Railway locomotive to be built, in January 1921: FR 4-6-4T (Baltic) No 119, possibly on a running-in turn, approaches Carnforth on a local train from Barrow. The two vans marshalled immediately behind the locomotive are Great Central Railway stock. *Bucknall Collection / Ian Allan Library*

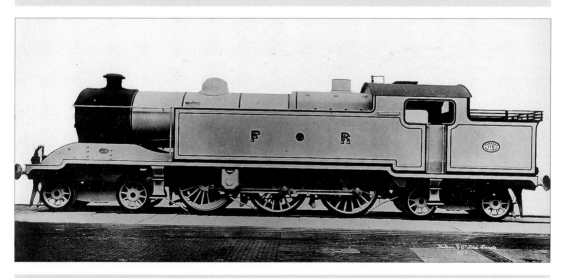

*Above:* The length and height of the FR 4-6-4Ts is well illustrated in this Kitson & Co works photograph of the first of the class, No 115, built in 1920. The class was the only inside-cylindered 4-6-4T design ever to run in Great Britain. *Bucknall Collection / Ian Allan Library*

## Whitehaven & Furness Junction Railway

There are conflicting accounts of the types of locomotives in W&FJ stock (owned jointly with the Whitehaven Junction Railway), all the product of northern locomotive builders, at the time of amalgamation with the FR in 1866. In previous books on the FR, both W. McGowan Gradon and R. W. Rush agree that the number of locomotives was 19, but differ on wheel arrangements (Rush's figures are shown in brackets):

| | |
|---|---|
| 0-4-2 | 4 (5) |
| 2-4-0 | 0 (2) |
| 0-6-0 | 6 (7) |
| 2-2-2T | 4 (3) |
| 0-4-0T | 2 (2) |
| unknown | 3 (0) |

Because certain W&FJ locomotives worked over the Whitehaven Junction Railway to Maryport and to Cockermouth through the joint ownership agreement, only nine locomotives passed to the FR in 1866, the remainder being handed to the London & North Western Railway.

Two of the 0-4-2s — Nos 3 and 13 — were renumbered 44 and 45 by the FR, and continued to work in West Cumberland until scrapping in 1882. 2-2-2 tank engines Nos 4 and 5 became FR Nos 47 and 48, but were of limited use on the Furness main line and were sold in 1870. Another 2-2-2 tank — No 10 — became FR No 46, and saw use on the Coniston and Lake Side branches until its sale to the Isle of Wight Central Railway in 1876. 0-6-0s Nos 19 and 18 became FR Nos 42 and 43, and were shedded at Whitehaven and Moor Row; No 42 had a long life, surviving until 1904. Finally, the two 0-4-0 saddle-tanks — Nos 15 and 16 — were renumbered as FR Nos 49 and 50, and continued to handle traffic between Preston Street goods depot, in Whitehaven, and the docks until 1882, when they were sold to a local engineering firm.

*Below:* Purchased from R. & W. Hawthorn in 1861, Whitehaven & Furness Junction Railway 2-2-2WT No 6 *Phoenix* (with attached tender displaying No 6) stands with a northbound train at St Bees. *Bucknall Collection / Ian Allan Library*

*Above:* Whitehaven & Furness Junction 0-4-2 No 3 *Mars*, built by R. & W. Hawthorn in 1857 and pictured at St Bees, where the church can just be seen on the far left. The date is probably the early 1860s, as the smokebox door is showing some wear, indicating a hard life. The FR renumbered the locomotive as No 44 in 1866, keeping it in service until 1882. *Bucknall Collection / Ian Allan Library*

*Above:* A Whitehaven & Furness Junction survivor: originally W&FJ No 19 and named *Lonsdale*, the locomotive was renumbered 42 by the FR. The photograph shows No 42 as rebuilt at Barrow in 1886: note that the locomotive has no cab, only front and rear weatherboards. *Bucknall Collection / Ian Allan Library*

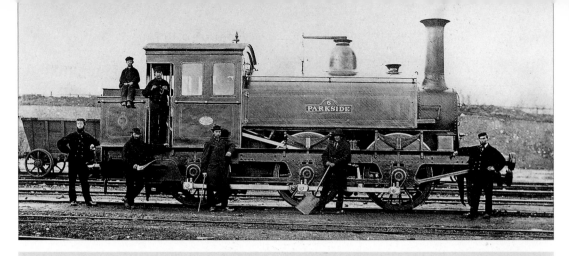

*Above:* Whitehaven, Cleator & Egremont 0-6-0ST No 6 *Parkside* of 1862, which became FR No 102 in 1878. This was the only member of the class, built by Robert Stephenson & Co, to have this totally-enclosed cab. The WC&E coat of arms can just be seen on the locomotive's bunker. A 'chaldron'-type iron-ore wagon can be seen behind the figure to the left of the locomotive. *Bucknall Collection / Ian Allan Library*

*Below:* WC&E No 4 *Keekle*, in original condition, which later became FR No 100. This locomotive had the distinction of having been built locally, in 1858, by Fletcher, Jennings & Co of Whitehaven. Note the crudely-built cab. *LPC*

### Whitehaven, Cleator & Egremont Railway

When the WC&E was absorbed by the Furness and the LNWR in 1879, the company had 17 locomotives on its books, 14 of which were 0-6-0 saddle-tanks. All the locomotives passed into FR stock, except for No 16, which was taken over by the LNWR and used for a time as works shunter at Crewe.

The 0-6-0 saddle-tanks became FR Nos 98 to 107 and 109 to 112, and WC&E 2-4-0 side-tank No 12 (the only outside-cylindered locomotive ever owned by the FR) was renumbered 108. After the latter was scrapped in 1898, the number was reallocated to 0-6-0ST No 112 in 1904. WC&E No 3 — a 0-6-0 side-tank — became FR No 113, until being sold out of service in 1898. The new No 108 was the last survivor of WC&E stock, passing into LMS ownership until scrapping in 1925.

*Below:* FR 0-6-0ST No 106, after rebuilding from WC&E No 10 *Crummock*. Unusually, this locomotive was built with a semi-circular saddle tank and without a cab, although one was added later. *LPC / Bucknall Collection*

*Below:* With lined-out livery, an immaculate FR 0-6-0ST No 105, formerly WC&E No 9 *Lowes Water*. Note the squared-off saddle tank, the large cab, the flared top to the bunker, and the two sets of buffers, for handling conventional and 'chaldron'-type wagons. The track on which the locomotive is standing has keys on the inside chairs. *Bucknall Collection / Ian Allan Library*

*Above:* The last survivor of the class: FR 0-6-0ST No 109A, formerly WC&E No 13 *Springfield* and now on the duplicate list, is pictured around the time of the 1923 Grouping. The livery is now unlined, the bunker has straight sides, and the locomotive has only one set of buffers. Withdrawal was in 1925. *LPC*

*Below:* FR 0-6-0ST No 108A, rebuilt in 1896 and 1915 from WC&E No 17 *Wastwater*. This differed from the previous 0-6-0STs in being built by Andrew Barclay, Sons & Co and in having inside frames. This was the last surviving WC&E locomotive, being withdrawn in 1925. *LPC*

94

# Classification of Furness Railway Locomotives

| Class | Wheel Arrangement | Type | Built | Original Numbers | Number in Class | Builder | Notes |
|---|---|---|---|---|---|---|---|
| A1 | 0-4-0 | Tender | 1844 | 1, 2 | 2 | Bury, Curtis & Kennedy | |
| A2 | 0-4-0 | Tender | 1846 | 3, 4 | 2 | Bury, Curtis & Kennedy | |
| A3 | 0-4-0 | Tender | 1854/5 | 7-10 | 4 | W. Fairbairn | |
| A4 | 0-4-0 | Tender | 1858-61 | 13-16 | 4 | W. Fairbairn | |
| A5 | 0-4-0 | Tender | 1863-6 | 17-20, 25-28 | 8 | Sharp, Stewart & Co | |
| B1 | 2-2-2 | Well-tank | 1852 | 5, 6 | 2 | Sharp Bros | |
| B2 | 2-2-2 | Well-tank | 1857 | 11, 12 | 2 | Sharp Bros | |
| B3 | 2-2-2 | Well-tank | 1864-6 | 21, 22, 34-37 | 6 | Sharp, Stewart & Co | |
| B4 | 2-2-2 | Well-tank | 1860 | 46 | 1 | R. & W. Hawthorn | Ex-W&FJR No 10 |
| B5 | 2-2-2 | Well-tank | 1850 | 47, 48 | 2 | E. B. Wilson | Ex-W&FJR Nos 4, 5 |
| C1 | 0-4-0 | Saddle-tank | 1864-74 | 23, 24, 94-97 | 6 | Sharp, Stewart & Co | |
| C2 | 0-4-0 | Saddle-tank | 1862 | 49 | 1 | Fletcher, Jennings & Co | Ex-W&FJR No 15 |
| | | | | 50 | 1 | Neilson & Co | Ex-W&FJR No 16 |
| D1 | 0-6-0 | Tender | 1866-83 | 17-20, 25, 26, 29-33, 38-41, 43, 49, 50, 53-56, 59-67, 76-81, 84-93, 114-121 | 55 | Sharp, Stewart & Co | Nicknamed 'Sharpies' |
| D2 | 0-6-0 | Tender | 1864 | 42, 43 | 2 | R. & W. Hawthorn | Ex-W&FJR Nos 18, 19 |
| D3 | 0-6-0 | Tender | 1899 | 7-12 | 6 | Nasmyth, Wilson & Co | |
| | | | | 13-18 | 6 | Sharp, Stewart & Co | |
| D4 | 0-6-0 | Tender | 1907 | 3-6 | 4 | North British Locomotive Co | |
| D5 | 0-6-0 | Tender | 1913-20 | 1, 2, 23-35 | 15 | North British Locomotive Co | |
| | | | | 19-22 | 4 | Kitson & Co | |
| E1 | 2-4-0 | Tender | 1870-82 | 1, 2, 5, 6, 11, 12, 44-48, 57, 58, 70-75 | 19 | Sharp, Stewart & Co | Seven converted to 2-4-2 side-tanks in 1891 |
| F1 | 0-4-2 | Tender | 1857 | 44, 45 | 2 | R. & W. Hawthorn | Ex-WFJR Nos 3, 13 |
| G1 | 0-6-0 | Side-tank | 1867-73 | 51, 52, 68, 69, 82, 83 | 6 | Sharp, Stewart & Co | Nicknamed 'Neddies' |
| G2 | 0-6-0 | Saddle-tank | 1855-73 | 98, 99, 101-107, 109-111 | 12 | Robert Stephenson | Ex-WC&ER Nos 1, 2, 5-11, 13-15 |
| | | | | 100 | 1 | Fletcher, Jennings & Co | Ex-WC&ER No 4 |
| G3 | 0-6-0 | Saddle-tank | 1875 | 112 | 1 | Andrew Barclay & Sons | Ex-WC&ER No 17 |
| G4 | 0-6-0 | Side-tank | 1857 | 113 | 1 | R. & W. Hawthorn | Ex-WC&ER No 3 |
| G5 | 0-6-0 | Side-tank | 1910-6 | 19-24, 53, 54 | 8 | Vulcan Foundry | |
| | | | | 51, 52 | 2 | Kitson & Co | |
| H1 | 2-4-0 | Side-tank | 1850 | 108 | 1 | Stothert & Slaughter | Ex-WC&ER No 12 |
| K1 | 4-4-0 | Tender | 1891 | 120-123 | 4 | Sharp, Stewart & Co | Nicknamed 'Seagulls' |
| K2 | 4-4-0 | Tender | 1896-1900 | 21, 22, 34-37, 124, 125 | 8 | Sharp, Stewart & Co | |
| K3 | 4-4-0 | Tender | 1901 | 126-129 | 4 | Sharp, Stewart & Co | |
| K4 | 4-4-0 | Tender | 1913/4 | 130-133 | 4 | North British Locomotive Co | |
| L1 | 0-6-2 | Side-tank | 1898 | 112-114 | 3 | Sharp, Stewart & Co | |
| L2 | 0-6-2 | Side-tank | 1904 | 98-102 | 5 | Nasmyth, Wilson & Co | |
| | | | | 103-107 | 5 | North British Locomotive Co | |
| L3 | 0-6-2 | Side-tank | 1907 | 96, 97, 108-111 | 6 | North British Locomotive Co | |
| L4 | 0-6-2 | Side-tank | 1912-4 | 92-95 | 4 | Kitson & Co | |
| M1 | 4-4-2 | Side-tank | 1915/6 | 38, 39, 42, 43 | 4 | Kitson & Co | |
| | | | | 40, 41 | 2 | Vulcan Foundry | |
| N1 | 4-6-4 | Side-tank | 1920/1 | 115-119 | 5 | Kitson & Co | Nicknamed 'Jumbos' |
| Unclass. | 0-4-0 | Railmotor | 1904/5 | 1, 2 | 2 | Furness Rly, Barrow Works | |

TOTAL FR-OWNED LOCOMOTIVES   242

Note: The Furness Railway had no official system for classifying its locomotives, relying purely on locomotive numbers for identification. The system shown above, based on wheel arrangements, is generally attributed to the late A. C. W. Lowe, who was not employed by the Furness Railway.

# Acknowledgements and Bibliography

I have received much help in the preparation of this volume, from many quarters, but would particularly like to thank Aidan Jones and his staff at the Cumbria Record Office, Barrow, as well as the Cumbria Record Office, Kendal. Tim Owen and Jim Kay, of the Furness Railway Trust, provided excellent photographs and reproduction postcards respectively, while John Broughton of the Cumbrian Railways Association produced a wide range of photographs at relatively short notice. Last but not least, my thanks to Ken Norman for keeping me up to date with information on other Furness Railway publishing activity, both in print and proposed.

The following publications have been particularly useful in preparing this volume:

*Early Railway History in Furness*, by J. Melville & J. L. Hobbs, published by Titus Wilson, 1951;

*Furness Railway: Its Rise & Development, 1846–1923*, by W. McGowan Gradon, published by the author, 1946;

*Furness and the Industrial Revolution*, by J. D. Marshall, published by Barrow Library & Museum Committee, 1958;

*The Furness Railway, 1843–1923*, by R. W. Rush, published by Oakwood Press, 1973;

*Furness Railway Locomotives & Rolling Stock*, by R. W. Rush, published by Oakwood Press, 1973;

'The Furness Railway & the Growth of Barrow', by S. Pollard and J. D. Marshall, published in the *Journal of Transport History*, Vol 1, No 2, November 1953;

*The Furness Railway: A Recollection*, by K. J. Norman, published by Silver Link Publishing, 1994;

*Cumbrian Coast Railways*, by David Joy, published by Dalesman Publishing Co, 1968;

*Regional History of the Railways of Great Britain: The Lake Counties*, by David Joy, published by David & Charles, 1983;

*Barrow & District: An Illustrated History*, by F. Barnes, published by Barrow Corporation, 1968;

*Branch Lines*, by O. S. Nock, published by B. T. Batsford, 1957;

*The Coniston Railway*, by Michael Andrews & others, published by Cumbrian Railways Association, 1985;

*Burlington Blue-Grey: A History of the Slate Quarries, Kirkby-in-Furness*, by R. Stanley Geddes, published by the author, 1975;

*Passengers No More*, by Gerald Daniels & L. A. Dench, published by Ian Allan, 1973;

*Bradshaw's Railway Guide*, April 1910;

*Bradshaw's Railway Guide*, July 1922;

*Railway Magazine* (various editions);

*Furness Railway Magazine*, Vols 1-3.

**Cumbrian Railways Association**
For any reader wishing to join the Cumbrian Railways Association, the Membership Secretary can be contacted at:

>36 Clevelands Avenue
>Barrow-in-Furness
>Cumbria
>LA13 0AE

**Furness Railway Trust**
The Secretary of the Furness Railway Trust can be contacted at:

>'Greystones'
>Mount Pleasant
>Greenodd
>Cumbria
>LA12 7RF

# THE FURNESS RAILWAY & SURROUNDING LINES

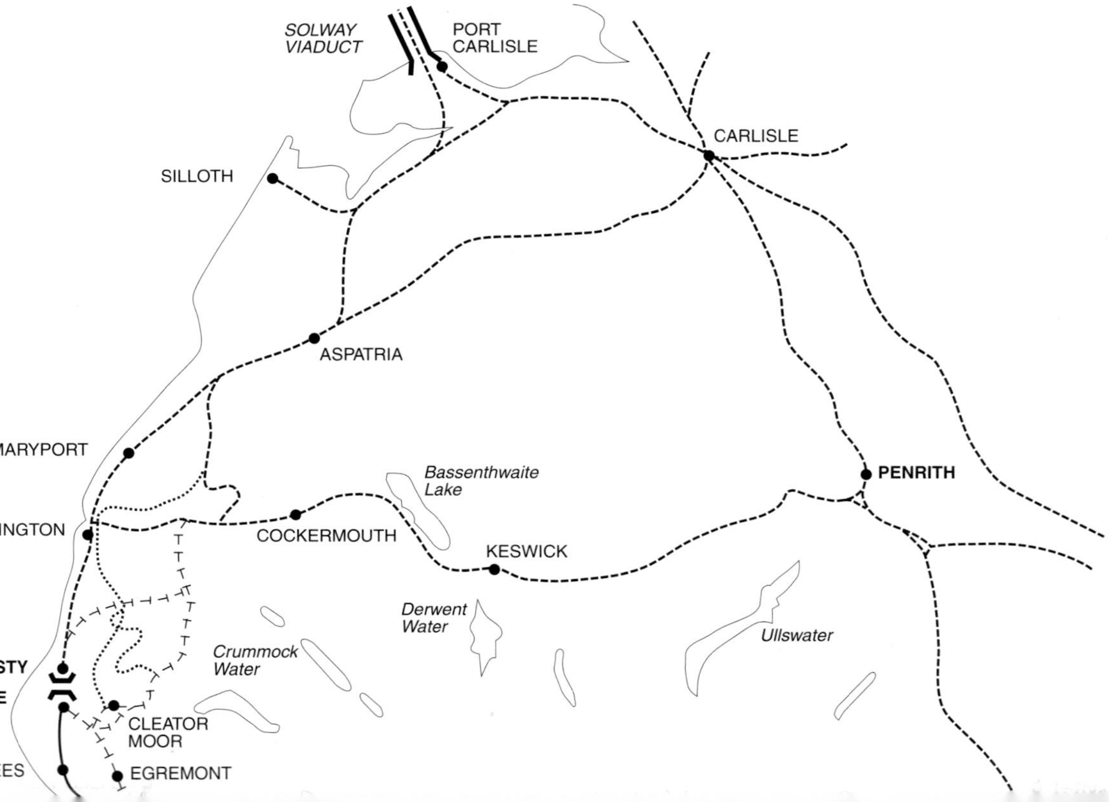

CARLISLE

PENRITH

Ullswater

PORT
CARLISLE

SOLWAY
VIADUCT

ASPATRIA

SILLOTH

Bassenthwaite
Lake

KESWICK

Derwent
Water

COCKERMOUTH

MARYPORT

Crummock
Water

WORKINGTON

CLEATOR
MOOR

EGREMONT

WHITEHAVEN BRANSTY
WHITEHAVEN CORKICKLE

SAINT BEES